"Gailus's Manifesto is an up-to-date indictment of our failure as westerners to protect the utlimate symbol of wilderness, and makes hollow our claim to be a unique citizenry with a special connection to the land. Gailus delivers a left hook to Parks Canada's bogus claims to put conservation ahead of tourist development, and gives a well deserved right cross to our cynical Alberta Government, which seems bent on letting grizzly bears blink out into oblivion. If you care about wild bears and wild lands, read this book."

—Sid Marty, author of *The Black Grizzly of Whiskey Creek*

"Like the roar of an angry bear, this book should set your pulse racing. Jeff Gailus weaves science, policy and personal experience into a passionate and provocative critique of Canada's failed efforts to halt the decline of the grizzly bear."

—David R. Boyd, environmental lawyer, professor, activist and author of *Unnatural Law: Rethinking Canadian Environmental Law and Policy*

The Grizzly Manifesto

In Defence
OF THE
Great Bear

Jeff Gailus

RMB
Victoria Vancouver Calgary

Rocky Mountain Books
www.rmbooks.com

Library and Archives Canada Cataloguing in Publication

Gailus, Jeff
    The grizzly manifesto / Jeff Gailus.

Includes bibliographical references.
ISBN 978-1-897522-83-7

    1. Grizzly bear—North America. 2. Grizzly bear—Conservation—North America. I. Title.

QL737.C27G34 2010   599.784'097   C2009-907203-3

Printed and bound in Canada

Rocky Mountain Books gratefully acknowledges the financial support of the Government of Canada Book Fund (CBF); the Canada Council for the Arts; and the province of British Columbia through the British Columbia Arts Council and the Book Publishing Tax Credit for our publishing activities.

 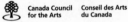

The interior pages of this book have been produced on 100% post-consumer recycled paper, processed chlorine free and printed with vegetable-based dyes.

For Makaila,
who inspires me always
to make the world a better place.

For all those who have committed their lives
to protecting and restoring grizzly bears
wherever they still roam.

And for Mary and 56:
may their deaths not have been in vain.

Contents

Acknowledgements

This book would not have been possible without the help and support of innumerable people. My family, for one, has been an indefatigable supporter of my dream to be a writer and change-maker, no matter how crazy and impractical it has seemed at times. Fred and Andrea, Chris and Jane, Erika and Paul, Alison and Laurent, Jennifer and Makaila, to you I owe everything.

Likewise, my dear friends Jim and Val Pissot and Peter and Diane Zimmerman. You have provided shelter in every storm, which has allowed me the freedom and flexibility to roam western North America in search of bears and dreams.

Ylva Lekberg, your patience and emotional support while I turned my rough draft into a manuscript was simply amazing. I couldn't have done it without you.

Thanks, too, to the Environmental Studies Program at the University of Montana, where

I learned how to blend science, policy and creativity into literature. Phil Condon, Dr. Dan Flores, Dr. Chris Servheen and Doug Chadwick, who sat on my thesis committee at U of M, thanks for having faith in me.

Bears are complex beings. Without the help of Dr. Michael Gibeau, Dr. Stephen Herrero, Dr. Dave Mattson, Dr. Scott Nielsen, Dr. Michael Proctor, Gordon Stenhouse and Louisa Willcox, I'd still be roaming around in the depths of ignorance. Much gratitude for the tutelage.

Don Gorman and Neil Wedin at RMB | Rocky Mountain Books, thanks for believing in me. Much gratitude, too, to Shauna Rusnak, the gifted editor who helped turn my garbled grammar into flowing prose. I look forward to working with all of you to make the *Manifesto Series* the best in its class.

I would be remiss if I didn't mention the various organizations and foundations that have provided financial support over the years, allowing me to study bears and the social and political machinations that determine their fates: the Alberta Foundation for the Arts, the Canada Council for the Arts, the Doris Duke Conservation Fellowship Program, the University of Montana's Matthew Hansen Endowment, the Yellowstone to Yukon Conservation Initiative and the Wilburforce Foundation.

I have no doubt forgotten numerous people who deserve to be on this page. My apologies, but I'm sure you know who you are. Thanks for all your direct and indirect support over the years.

Lastly, thank you to the bears themselves, who have allowed me innumerable glimpses into their world, and provided a guide of sorts to help navigate the mad, mad world we call civilization.

Jeff Gailus
Canmore, Alberta

Hunting for Grizzlies

Near Yellowstone National Park, 2001: I wake up in the cold and the dark of my Cooke City motel room, the air redolent of two-stroke oil and gasoline. Cooke City, on the eastern edge of Yellowstone National Park, is more village than city. Every winter it is overrun by thrill-seeking snowmobilers, some of whom had obviously used my room as a repair shop. I stumble around for the light switch and immediately put on a pot of coffee before hunting the oil-stained carpet for my clothes. It's 5:23. I have seven minutes to get ready. We're on the hunt for grizzlies.

Louisa Willcox had invited me to attend her annual media tour to learn about the plight of Yellowstone's grizzlies, a population of 600 or so bears that has been listed as endangered since 1975. Now that the population has more than tripled in size, the US government wants to remove the protections afforded it by the US Endangered Species Act. Willcox believes, with the conviction of an evangelical preacher, that this move is a mistake.

As a lowly reporter at a weekly newspaper in Canmore, Alberta, I often covered the lives and deaths of grizzly bears in and around Banff National Park. Willcox, on the other hand, is the grande dame of grizzly bear conservation in North America. Thin and wiry-strong, the former monkey-wrencher and National Outdoor Leadership School (NOLS) guide has more energy than a wolverine. She has worked to protect Yellowstone's grizzly bears for more than 25 years. When Willcox found out I often wrote about bears and the politics that decide their fates, she thought I should come down to witness what was happening in Yellowstone.

To my great dismay, I had learned the night before at the "meet and greet" that the best time to locate Yellowstone's more mythical beasts is during the auroral hinge that joins night and day. Despite my vampire-like aversion to early morning wake-up calls, I manage to find my way into the parking lot before the last vehicle has left. I stumble into a red minivan driven by a genial documentary filmmaker from Bozeman, Montana. As we pull onto US212 in the tepid daylight, I take a long pull on the coffee steaming from my travel mug. Ten minutes later, we are in the park. As we approach our destination – a roadside pullout near the carcass of a bison killed by wolves the day before – a coyote dashes across the road and a golden eagle glides insouciantly over the car. It feels like we are on an African safari.

We pull over and climb the steep path onto a hillside that offers a spectacular view of the entire valley. At six o'clock on a May morning, the Lamar Valley is blissfully quiet. Through our spotting scopes, we see camouflaged elk browsing the high ridges on the far side of the valley. Closer to hand, Soda Butte Creek meanders through this wide, flat basin with the rhythmic beat of a metronome set slow. Big, dark bison crop new-growth grass on the far bank, and sandhill cranes stand stock-still in the shallows, hunting. Only a meadowlark dares break the stillness with its flutish song.

More than two dozen "watchers" bundle thick against the cool morning air for the chance to see a grizzly bear or a wolf. We are part of an annual pilgrimage to the mecca of accessible American wilderness. People journey here, hundreds of them, from all over Canada and the United States to answer a deep-seated desire to connect with wildness. For many, it has become an obsession.

"We've been comin' here, oh, 15-odd years now," says one of the watchers, a 74-year-old retired rancher named Les Smith, pointing to his wife, Clare. "We've watched [some of Yellowstone's] bears since they was cubs."

Among us, too, are the filmmakers, journalists and writers that have come for the media tour – some from as far away as Los Angeles, some from such prestigious magazines as *Time*. Several well-known wildlife biologists are also here to act as our guides and expert witnesses as we muddle our way through the biology and politics of grizzly bear conservation.

A shout breaks the still morning air. One of the watchers has spotted wolves. Four members of the Druid Peak pack trot west along Soda Butte Creek before huddling around a dark shape 500 metres from our vantage point. They have found the bison carcass and all lean down to rip and tug at what I imagine is frozen flesh. They take turns lifting their heads to survey the valley, looking and smelling for anything that might usurp their caloric bonanza.

A few minutes later, another shout announces a grizzly sow and her three yearling cubs lumbering eastward toward the wolves. The sow is dark brown, her guard hairs tipped with the grey-gold that gives these bears their "grizzled" look. Her cubs are the size of domestic dogs. They are all hungry.

Behind me, the biologists banter back and forth like mill workers arguing about which team will win the Stanley Cup. On one side are the "risk takers," who think the sow, only recently out of the den and famished after a foodless winter, might just challenge the wolves for the much-needed protein. On the other side are the "risk avoiders," who conclude (rather emphatically, it seems to me, given the uncertain circumstances) that the sow's concern for the safety of her cubs will lead her to forsake the opportunity to pilfer the prize from the much smaller wolves. One voice confidently says that as an organic whole, a healthy wolf pack sits firmly atop the food chain here. They have been known to attack, even kill, grizzly bears.

I am astonished to learn that anything but a high-powered rifle or a speeding vehicle could kill a grizzly bear. After all, grizzly bears *did* win out over sabre-toothed tigers and a whole horde of fierce competitors who vanished when humans showed up in North America about 11,000 years ago. In fact, grizzlies arrived 15,000 years *before* humans; their bad tempers and poker-faced bluff charges allowed them to thrive in a world full of giant short-faced bears, American lions and packs of dire wolves much larger than this one. Less confident in my predictions than the scientists, I keep my thoughts to myself and just sit, watch and listen. Grizzlies are nothing if not resilient, though, so with quiet confidence I know I side with the bears.

At first it seems the "risk avoiders" are right about the mother bear's caution. The sow and her cubs pass within 15 metres of the wolf-covered carcass, but it does not appear as though she intends to challenge the wolves. The grizzly doesn't even seem to look at them as she waddles by, though the black wolf, his head hung low, watches her with a vigilance reserved for the wise or the fearful.

"See?" boasts the confident voice behind me. "I told you. No way. It's too risky."

As the word "risky" trails off into the wind, the sow whirls around and charges the wolves with the speed and intensity of a middle linebacker blitzing an unprotected quarterback, her cubs following close behind her. When she reaches the dark mound of dead bison, the wolves scatter like leaves in the wind. She climbs atop the carcass and whirls this way and that to face them, each wolf taking a turn to dart in and nip at her or grab a cub. She whirls and whirls, while the cubs plaster themselves to their mother's gyrating haunch, hoping she can fend off the wolves.

After a few swats of her giant paws, the wolves relent. They are patient, if nothing else, and there is time. They hunker down in the long grass to watch the grizzly quartet tear bright red flesh from white bones. She has won the carcass, at least for now.

This is a relatively new experience for Yellowstone grizzly bears. Grizzlies didn't have to deal with these canine competitors between 1935, when wolves were eliminated from the American West, and 1996, when wildlife biologists reintroduced 14 wolves into a national park overrun by elk. During that time, the bears simply helped themselves to the winter-killed bison and elk, which created something of a spring buffet for them.

Now the park's 600 grizzlies must compete with some 170 wolves for these gifts of winter. Of course, grizzlies now also have the opportunity to cash in on wolf kills. In fact, some biologists believe that wolf kills usurped by grizzly bears more than compensate for the loss of winterkilled meat. Besides, they argue, such is the nature of things. This is as it should be.

For 30 minutes, nothing changes. The wolves are all but invisible in the long grass and the four bears continue to bolt down meat. But then something strange happens. Far to the east, another black wolf moves briskly toward the scene. It's as if the pack has called for re-inforcements. The new wolf crosses the creek, sending a handful of elk skittering through the grass. When he is within 100 feet of the carcass, his pack-mates rise from their hiding places in the tall grass and hurry to join him. The feeding bears don't seem to notice. The wolves worry together for more than a minute, touching noses and communicating, somehow, in an unspoken language beyond our ken. And then they wheel toward the carcass, scattering the bears like leaves.

The sow and her cubs begin to walk away, back the way they had come, west toward Specimen Ridge. We too prepare to leave. Not because we are bored of this spectacle, but because we have a series of presentations to give (if you're a biologist) and attend (if you're a journalist) at a ranch more than an hour's drive away. When everyone else has left, I linger, unable to tear myself away from a story that doesn't seem to have reached its natural conclusion.

I look to my right and notice I am not alone. I introduce myself, and my companion does likewise. He's David Quammen, one of the United States' most celebrated nature writers. Our hands tucked in our coat pockets against the cold, we chat and watch the wolves watching the bears. I mention that I have been visiting Banff National Park and the southern Canadian Rockies my whole life, but I've never seen as much wildlife as I have this morning. I had always thought of Canada as the great land of wilderness and wildlife, yet here we were, almost smack dab in the middle of the continental United States, surrounded by a multitude of predators and prey interacting as they might have 300 years ago. It is as if we have travelled back in time, before the coming of our European antecedents. By comparison, Canada's Rocky Mountain national parks seemed like deserts.

Quammen, well-versed in all things wild, simply nods his head. He lives in Bozeman and comes here often. What I have only just come to realize is no surprise to him.

We start down the path together, Quammen and I, but stop for one last glimpse before we drop to the road. The sow stops in her tracks, too, and turns back to the wolves. She is perhaps 90 metres away. She stands up on her hind legs, rising for a better look. Dropping down on all fours, she turns her head to look west, weighing the probability of finding something equally nutritious elsewhere against the energy and risk it will take to recapture the carcass. Then she sweeps her massive skull back toward the wolves and charges the carcass, her cubs trailing behind her, the wolves scattering and the eternal dance continuing with no end in sight.

A Grizzly Education

We were greeted at the B-Bar Ranch by a gourmet lunch buffet and a life-sized statue of a grizzly bear. The B-Bar is a 9,000-acre (3600-hectare) ranch in the Tom Miner Basin, on the northern boundary of Yellowstone National Park. Unlike many ranches, the B-Bar is a wildlife-friendly place, where the elk, moose, bears and wolves wander at will. I can attest to this generosity personally. On a subsequent visit, I spooked a herd of more than 100 elk, which thundered past me like a herd of feral mustangs. The next day, on a short walk out behind the main building, I almost stepped on a chocolate brown grizzly bear hiding in the sagebrush hunting elk calves. I just about shit my pants. While I froze statue-still, he leapt up and ran 200 metres to the nearest copse of trees with the speed of a thoroughbred. All I saw was a bear ass for about 10 seconds and then he disappeared, as if the whole incident were nothing more than a dream.

The B-Bar is also a Friend of the Earth, allowing environmentalists like Willcox to host events that help to protect bears and other wildlife. Willcox had arranged for several biologists to come and educate us on the biology and status of grizzly bears in western North America. Some were independent experts concerned about the future of grizzly bears, such as Paul Paquet, Michael Proctor and Lance Craighead – the son of one of the famous Craighead brothers, who pioneered grizzly-bear research in Yellowstone. At least one participant worked for the government; he had come under cover of darkness to tell us what he knew. Conspicuously absent was Chris Servheen, who has coordinated grizzly bear recovery for the US government for almost 30 years. It seems he and Willcox have something of a feud going. I couldn't help feeling like there was a conspiracy afoot and that we were being groomed to blow it wide open.

The biologists' job was to present their research and use their professional judgment to fill the many gaps that exist in what we know about grizzly bears. The picture was rather bleak. Grizzly bears roamed most of North America until 250 years ago. Since the arrival of white men, with poison and increasingly lethal rifles, grizzly bear range has shrunk north and west. By 1930, the Great Bear had been relegated to little islands of mountainous habitat in the western US, a thin sliver of western Alberta, BC, and the Canadian North. Today, Alberta's grizzly population has dwindled to less than 700; BC hosts about 15,000; and Nunavut, the Yukon and Northwest Territories harbour fewer than 10,000.

The Greater Yellowstone Ecosystem (GYE) is one island of grizzly habitat. Anchored at the centre by the world's first national park, the GYE is also home to a growing number of loggers, hunters, snowmobilers, ranchers, tourists and second-home owners. By 1975, when all grizzlies in the lower 48 states were listed as endangered, the Yellowstone grizzly bear population had dropped to a mere 200 animals. With the full force of the Endangered Species Act behind them, environmentalists forced the US Fish & Wildlife Service to do a better job of ensuring a future for Yellowstone's grizzly bears. Now there are more than 600 grizzlies in the GYE, so the United States government wants to declare success and take the Yellowstone grizzly off the endangered species list. Willcox thinks otherwise, and she is encouraging the environmental community and anyone else she can convince to oppose delisting at all costs. Which is why, of course, we are here.

Most of the biologists didn't express an opinion either way, but they did seem to think that from a biological point of view there are plenty of problems to iron out before the population can be declared recovered. There is concern that some of the grizzlies' primary food sources in Yellowstone are at risk of disappearing in the very near future, particularly white-bark pine nuts and cutthroat trout. Other concerns are that the population might still be too small, which puts it at risk of inbreeding, or that climate change would fundamentally change the nature of the landscape. Willcox is convinced that without the protection of the Endangered Species Act, humans will become too damn lethal again. In addition, several other populations on the US–BC border are precariously small, isolated and in desperate need of some attention from the US Fish & Wildlife Service.

By the end of the day, I couldn't help but wonder what the hell the US government was thinking. While a threefold increase in bears seems pretty damn impressive, the list of problems still on the table seems inordinately long. As I helped myself to my third plate of smoked salmon and another glass of the peppery cabernet, it seemed to me that we had done a pretty good job of managing our grizzly bears in Canada. Perhaps we needed to come down and show them how to get the job done.

The next morning I ate my words, or at least my thoughts, for breakfast. It was Brian Horejsi's turn to speak and what he had to say shocked me more than what I had heard the day before. Brian is an outspoken grizzly-bear biologist from Alberta, of all places. In fact, he lives less than 100 kilometres from my house, which by Canadian standards is just around the corner. I had travelled all the way to Yellowstone to learn the truth about grizzly bears at home.

The gist was this: do not count on Canadian grizzly bears to cross the border and buoy up US populations. If anything, grizzly bears are probably moving from the US, where they are protected, into Canada, where they are being recklessly killed and mismanaged. In fact, he said, Alberta likely has fewer grizzly bears than Montana or Wyoming and the population is in deep trouble.

On the plane ride home, I watched what was left of Grizzly Country scroll by beneath me like a filmstrip. I couldn't help but think about the grizzly sow and her three cubs, fighting for survival in one of the *safest* places to be a grizzly bear in all of North America. If what I had heard were true, things were much worse in Canada. Clear-cuts, roads, seismic lines, oil wells, gas pipelines and rednecks with ATVs and guns are making it all but impossible for grizzly bears to eke out a living in the forests, foothills and alpine meadows that we haven't yet taken away from them. They are dying of collisions with trucks and trains, gunshot wounds and poison faster than they can reproduce. We are pushing them out of every place where our hard work and ingenuity has discovered something valuable, like coal, hot springs or cattle-supporting grass. More than 100 years after we invented the concepts of "protected areas" and "wildlife conservation," the overheated engine of techno-industrial Progress is still driving the bears north and west like cattle. And now, whether I liked it or not, I felt obligated to do something about it.

A Place for People and Bears

Change comes slowly. It took me two years to make good on my promise to help make the world a better place for grizzly bears. A few months after my trip to Yellowstone, I quit my job at the *Canmore Leader,* trading indentured servitude for the uncertainty of freelancing. I also began guiding people into the mountains and along the West Coast Trail, teaching them not only about the natural world, but also about how to relate to it in ways they aren't used to in their urban homes.

If we were lucky, we would encounter the occasional grizzly bear, usually along the Trans-Canada Highway or at the snowless Lake Louise ski hill we used as a gateway to

Banff's backcountry. At every sighting, the bear drew oohs and aahs from my middle-aged charges as they rushed to raise their cameras before the bear disappeared into the bush. The symbolic power of the Great Bear walking upon the earth, as it once had with mammoths, mastodons and our Neanderthal cousins, fulfilled their dreams and ineluctably changed their worlds.

Part fear, part awe, these rarefied experiences were always the highlights of their trips. In part, I think, it was the fulfillment of a hope that they might see such a mythical beast with their own eyes. The merest glimpse of a grizzly always seemed to defy even their highest expectations. Like having a child, encountering a grizzly bear in the wild is something you can anticipate with the common sense of the conscious mind, but when it finally arrives, you discover one of the few experiences that actually surpass what you had imagined. It felt, at least for some of them, like a gift from God.

In November, I landed a full-time job with the Yellowstone to Yukon Conservation

Initiative (Y2Y), an exciting new conservation organization that had opened an office in Canmore. Charged with looking after their outreach and communications needs, I spent most of my time trying to convince people that our idea was a good one.

The idea behind Y2Y is relatively simple: despite the usual challenges – industrial activity (particularly forestry and oil and gas), major highways, dams, towns, cities and millions of people – the Rocky Mountain landscape from Canada's northern Yukon to the Greater Yellowstone Ecosystem is still relatively healthy. In this 1.3-million-square-kilometre region, the air is clean and most of the rivers are unpolluted and unobstructed. Unlike most of the other great mountain ranges in the world, the Rockies still contain the full complement of native species that Alexander Mackenzie or Lewis and Clark might have encountered when they travelled through on their way west. Although some species teeter on the edge, Y2Y argues that if we put our heads together and play our cards right, there is still a chance we can keep this unique landscape healthy and whole.

The grizzly bear, which adorns the organization's logo, is at the heart of this idea. Provide for the needs of the grizzly bear, the logic goes, and you will maintain an ecosystem healthy enough to support all its constituent parts. It's not a foolproof assumption, but all other things being equal, focusing on a sensitive "umbrella" species like the grizzly is an effective way to ensure that water supplies stay clean and abundant and that birds, mammals and fish are protected.

Dr. Stephen Herrero is professor emeritus at the University of Calgary and one of the most pre-eminent grizzly bear experts in the world. He calls the grizzly bear an indicator of sustainable development. Like monarch butterflies and coral reefs, grizzly bears tell us whether the sum total of our activities are being conducted in ways that meet "the needs of the present without compromising the ability of future generations to meet their own needs." Where grizzly bears are allowed to continue to exist, our behaviour is sustainable. Where they are being extirpated, we are dipping into our natural capital and leaving the world a depleted shadow of itself for our children and grandchildren.

The reasons why grizzly bears are so sensitive to human disturbance are complex. For one thing, they require a huge amount of space. Being large terrestrial omnivores that eat (believe it or not) mostly plants, they require an extensive habitat to meet their dietary needs. In poor-quality habitat, the largest males can roam up to 1200 square kilometres a year in search of food. This home range will overlap with several females', but males really don't like to share space, food or females. That means a healthy population of grizzly bears, which should number in the hundreds if not the thousands to maintain long-term genetic health, requires tens of thousands of square kilometres to sustain itself.

Grizzly bears also reproduce very slowly. Most females only breed every three or four years and usually have only one or two cubs. Cub survival, especially in human-dominated landscapes, is low. Each female may replace herself only once or twice in her lifetime. There is very little margin for error. If human-caused mortalities are too high, as they have been since the repeating rifle replaced the muzzle loader in the mid-1800s, then grizzly bear populations shrink and shrink and shrink and eventually disappear. Like a shallow lake under a hot desert sun, the edges retreat toward the centre until one day it is totally and utterly gone.

The other part of the equation is that grizzly bears and people often find it hard to get along. Grizzly bears spend most of the winter hibernating, so when they are out and about, they are hard-wired to eat and eat and eat. They must eat a year's worth of food in eight months. When natural food sources run low – the berry crop fails, say, or the salmon do not return to spawn – they are inclined to kill cattle or raid barns, campgrounds or garbage for the calories they need to see them through hibernation.

Grizzlies are driven by the instinct of survival: if they do not put on enough fat before the snow comes, they will die in their dens. We, however, can alter our behaviour in relatively small ways that can prevent almost all human–bear conflicts. Securing our garbage and other unnatural food sources is most important, but we also need to leave enough undeveloped wilderness for bears to live their lives the only way they know how.

Grizzlies are also fearless defenders of their cubs and their food. Every once in awhile they attack and even kill someone, but such attacks are rare – rarer, say, than dying from a bee sting or a dog attack – and they are usually easily avoided or repelled. I have experienced this first-hand. My Y2Y colleagues and I travelled to the Elisi Wilderness Retreat, a backcountry lodge on the edge of the Muskwa–Kechika wilderness. We chose this particular place for our annual board meeting for the chance to experience one of North America's greatest remaining wilderness areas – what some people call the Serengeti of the North.

On our third morning, the board went in camera to discuss matters to which I, as an employee, was not privy. I was delighted. It was beautiful and sunny. After two days of airports and airplanes, plus two days of 14-hour meetings, my back was stiff and my mind was soft as ripe brie. It was time to venture into the woods, alone.

"Are you sure that's a good idea?" said my friend Jerry when I told him my plans over breakfast. "This is pretty wild country. Do you have bear spray?"

"No," I replied, "but I don't think I'll need it. I've been running in grizzly country all my life without it and I've never had a problem. Besides," I added with a grin, "if you've got to go, I can think of no better way than at the hands of a grizzly bear."

Jerry, who looks a lot like Santa Claus, sat on Y2Y's board at the time. He's a former logger turned conservationist and garden photographer from Bonners Ferry, Idaho. His specialty is roses, and his sincerity and generosity are unrivalled. Knowing my penchant for good single-malt Scotch, he had brought me a bottle of Lagavulin, the thick, peaty brew from the south coast of the Isle of Islay.

"Alright," he says, his gargantuan smile pulling his white beard up toward his eyes. "But if something does happen, can I have what's left of the Scotch?"

"Sure," I laugh. "It's all yours."

Outfitted in running shoes and shorts, I headed out along the log rail fence that rings the horse corral. I followed the trail worn hard by the hooves of pack horses as it snaked up the gentle slope, behind the lodge, through groves of aspen and across the open meadows. It was June in northern BC. The air was crisp and cool, despite the warmth of the mid-morning sun. A few cotton clouds waltzed across an azure sky, and yellow wildflowers – lousewort and cinquefoil among them – broke up a stunning wash of spring green. It was about as pastoral a scene as one could imagine in the depths of BC's backcountry wilderness.

Here and there, small herds of elk watched me intently. They were cows, mostly, followed closely by their skittish, exuberant calves, which still bore the white spots that would fade by fall. The calves crowded close to their mothers as I ambled past, my stride shortened by the steepening grade and the certainty of gravity. My chest soon began to heave and sweat trickled down the small of my back, but the trail soon levelled off, thank God, paralleling the ridgeline above me. I relaxed, following the undulating rhythm of the trail as it dropped into the many small creek beds cut into the hillside by uncountable spring runoffs. When I appeared suddenly on the low crests that separated them, apprehensive elk emitted loud barks and stampeded out of sight with their offspring in tow. It became something of a pattern, this undulation, which quickly lulled me into the gentle rhythm of complacency.

When I crested the next rise, another bark leapt into the stillness. This one was deeper and rumbly (as Pooh would say), perhaps more of a growl than a bark. I looked around, but there were no elk in sight. In units of time too small to measure, I started to compare the growl to various sounds from the previous 30 minutes. Suddenly a bear the colour of dark chocolate rushed out of a thick shock of alder 100 feet in front of me. The hair on its back stood up like hackles on a dog and its prominent shoulder hump indicated, in no uncertain terms, that it was a grizzly. Its eyes, small and dark, gleamed. It huffed loudly, a great woof. Its breath came out hard and measured, like a middle-distance runner pushing fast on the last lap.

Just when I thought things could get no worse, two small, dark cubs popped out of the bushes directly behind their mother, bobbing along like newborn puppies. I keenly felt like the wolves that I had watched trying to defend their breakfast in Yellowstone. As I stood alone on that hillside, an irate sow storming toward me with the quick, bowlegged gait of a bulldog accosting a stranger who has happened into its yard, my thoughts revert: I'm going to lose that bottle of Scotch.

It is unbelievable now, and more than a little disconcerting, to think that my initial reaction to 400 pounds of aggressive mother grizzly was centred on a half-empty bottle of alcohol, however fine. But we cannot always choose our thoughts; sometimes they simply

31

rise in the mind, like trout to the surface of a pool in a cold, rushing stream.

I stumbled backward a step or two, losing my mind completely, and looked around for anything to throw at her. Thankfully, there was not a rock in sight larger than a plum, for had I actually clunked her on the head I might just as easily incited rather than dissuaded her. Finally realizing that counterattack was futile and would likely only make matters worse, I turned to face her. Remembering what I had so often taught others, I raised my arms above my head. Then in an apologetic and obsequious tone, usually reserved for women and God, I reminded her why I was a threat so insignificant she should ignore any thoughts of killing me.

Whoa bear.

Whoa bear.

It's just me.

I have no quarrel with you.

I'm just minding my own business.

Whoa bear!

WHOA BEAR!

When all seemed lost and contact inevitable, she stopped. She was 20 feet away; a distance a bear can cover in less than a second. The two dark cubs fidgeted but she stood stock still, as if considering whether to simply knock me down or tear me into little pieces. The world was silent, but for the pounding of my heart and her heavy breathing, which I can hear even now as clearly as my own. She gave me a firm and knowing look, her dark eyes holding mine for a discernible moment. Then she turned and followed the trail over the next rise and out of sight, her cubs trailing obediently behind her. None of them even looked back.

Under the circumstances, I thought the bear showed a great deal of restraint. Had she attacked and injured (or killed) me, I would have wanted no retribution delivered on the bear. I knew better. I should not have been out alone in grizzly country and I should have been making enough noise to warn her of my presence. I should have been carrying bear spray. My well-being was my responsibility, not hers, and her aggressive response was strictly defensive. The saddest consideration is that had I been someone else, someone inclined to carry a rifle, I'm certain she would be dead and her cubs left to starve.

For every report of a grizzly bear attack or mauling, there are thousands of encounters between people and bears that end peacefully and add depth and meaning to people's lives. Despite the statistical harmlessness of bears, attacks do happen. When they do occur, the media strikes fear into our hearts because it is often our instinctive and unconscious fear (not our rational judgment) that sells newspapers and draws viewers. As a result, most people are irrationally afraid of grizzly bears. This keeps some of them out of bear habitat, which is probably a good thing. Mostly, though, it makes those who live, work and play there trigger-happy.

Conservation officers, in the interests of public safety and economic livelihood, routinely kill grizzly bears that frequent ranches, towns or garbage dumps. Hunters shoot them as trophies for the den floor or when they mistake them for black bears. Often the shooting is labelled self-defence: hiking quietly through the forest stalking deer, they surprise a sow with, say, two cubs. She charges. Rather than use bear-spray, which they might not have brought, they put a .30-calibre bullet in her chest. The cubs cannot survive without her, so now we have three dead bears. Poachers are the worst of the lot; like mercenaries and serial killers, they do their killing on the sly. It makes them feel powerful and cool, or they hate everything the grizzly bear represents – heavy-handed government, respect for the natural world, humility and restraint. Allegedly, some poachers earn as much as $3-million a year.

Many poaching deaths go undiscovered or unreported, but those revealed tend to raise the public ire. Such was the fate of Mary, a well-known and tolerant 7-year-old sow who lived in and around Jasper National Park. She frequented the sides of forestry roads when outside the protective boundaries of the park, eating grass, horsetails and dandelions.

Government biologists loved her because she proved that bears can and do live along roads, where locals from nearby Hinton, Alberta, often came to watch her feed, sometimes tossing her a box of doughnuts to help her through the winter. Biologists put an ear tag and a radio collar on her, to keep track of her movements as part of a research project.

One day in September, someone stumbled upon the rotting carcass of a grizzly bear. It wore no collar and its ears had been cut off, making it difficult to identify. Biologists suspected it was Mary, a hypothesis subsequent DNA evidence proved true.

A few weeks later, they found a small cooler floating in a nearby river. In it were Mary's tagged ears and radio collar. If a radio collar doesn't move for a specified period, it sends out a mortality signal that allows biologist to find it and its bearer. Mary's collar had been set adrift to make it seem like she was still alive and roaming the road-infested landscape for food. The local community was outraged and a substantial reward was posted for the apprehension of the perpetrator. Her killer was never found.

Mary's story, and hundreds of others just like it, tells us that grizzly bears do not survive where human activity is too intensive. History has proven this over the last 300 years, while a library of scientific research has confirmed it over the last 20 years. Despite overwhelming public support for grizzly bear conservation, in both Canada and the US, it has proven impossible to prevent grizzly bear deaths in places where there are too many people.

This is not to say that grizzly bears and people cannot coexist; they can. For example, national park policy precludes people from carrying guns, which makes it difficult for them to kill grizzly bears. At the same time, preventive measures – education, bear-proofed garbage bins, well-trained wardens and rangers – tend to prevent conflicts in the first place. But on unprotected, multiple-use lands where logging, mining, oil and gas exploration and hunting take place – i.e., most of grizzly bear habitat – it is hard to maintain grizzly bear populations.

The most effective way to sustain grizzly bear populations is to limit the number of roads in their habitat. Extensive research indicates that where the density of roads exceeds 0.6 kilometres per square kilometre (one mile per square mile), grizzly bears die faster than they can reproduce. Eventually, populations disappear altogether. The vast majority of grizzly bear deaths are caused by humans, and occur within 500 metres of a road, trail, cutline or seismic line – basically any place a 4x4 truck or ATV can navigate.

Although the majority of hunters, backpackers, well drillers, loggers, horsemen, trappers, guide–outfitters and ranchers work, live and play responsibly in grizzly country, a small percentage do not. They attract bears by leaving their food and garbage out, and then shoot them in reputed self-defence. Or, they misunderstand a bear's blustery behaviour and drop the animal with a clean shot to the lungs from 50 yards away. The rottenest of the bunch seek them out and shoot them on sight, big grins on their knuckleheaded faces. If we want grizzly bears to survive, the only answer is to limit the amount of motorized access by not building roads in what remains of our wilderness.

That was my job at Y2Y: to go out into the world and try to explain this in ways that might resonate with people, and maybe even inspire them to support us. The response wasn't always favourable. Fearful its access to timber was in jeopardy, the BC forestry industry mounted a slanderous PR campaign to convince people, both rural and urban, that Y2Y wanted to shut forestry down and turn the entire region into one big park – destroying all forestry-dependent communities in the process. Another myth had it that Y2Y was an American scheme cooked up by American environmentalists to lock up a large chunk of Canada. The same insane story began circulating in the US, except the evil plunderer was the United Nations, its operatives covertly shuttling about in black helicopters in an attempt to turn a country-sized chunk of North America into a wilderness playground for wealthy European diplomats. None of these stories were true, of course, but the neo-conservatives, libertarians and small-minded among us felt threatened by the power of a vision that challenged old paradigms that were no longer capable of serving society as a whole. Decades of scientific research were repeating (over and over again) some pretty inconvenient truths. It was time for something new.

Despite the fear-mongering, support grew. Dozens of foundations, citizen organizations and businesses cobbled themselves into a network. Well-informed policy-makers concerned about the extraordinary rate of biodiversity loss began to recognize Y2Y as one of the best examples of trying to find a balance between economic development and environmental protection. The United Nations Environmental Programme did this, as well as the Canadian government. The wheels were turning and the train was leaving the station. In my own small way, I felt like I was fulfilling my obligations to the grizzly bears I had learned about in Yellowstone.

I was helping people, particularly people who saw the world differently than I did, to understand what was at stake, what the problems were and how we might come together to solve them. It wasn't easy. The more I learned about the wounds we were inflicting upon the natural world, the harder it became to look the other way. Fifty years ago, Aldo Leopold wrote in *A Sand County Almanac* that this is one of the most painful penalties of an ecological education. Once we begin to understand the impacts of our collective behaviour, Leopold suggests, we "either harden our shells" and make believe the consequences are none of our business, or we become the doctor "who sees the marks of death in a community that believes itself well and does not want to be told otherwise."

I had not seen enough to feel Leopold's cynicism. I was still convinced that once people had the right information, they would surely come to the same rational conclusion I had: that it makes no sense to keep destroying the ecosystems upon which we depend. Once convinced, we could all go hand in hand to our elected officials and ask them to do the right thing, which, if we had done our research and made a strong case, they most surely would do.

The Remarkable Mister Grizzly

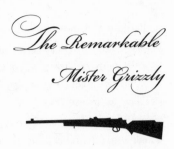

Grizzly bears are remarkable creatures that modern science has allowed us to learn some of the secrets of. For one thing, they are voracious eaters. A single grizzly bear can eat as many as 20,000 berries in a single day, its nimble lips capable of picking each berry without so much as disturbing a leaf. They eat anything and everything, from the flesh of great beasts to whitebark pine seeds cached by squirrels. While they are at it, they will eat the squirrels and their babies, too. They climb high up onto scree slopes and lick up army cutworm moths from over-turned rocks. But mostly, grizzly bears eat plants: berries, hedysarum roots, cow parsnip, horsetails and glacier lilies. Even grass.

Perhaps the most incredible part of their life cycle is their reproductive strategy. Grizzly bears mate in the spring, when hormonal males track down cubless females. The courtship can last days, even weeks, while the amorous couple plays and roughhouses. This foreplay brings the female into estrus, her body dropping an egg or two into place. Then they copulate again and again; the sex is interrupted by bouts of feeding and resting, sometimes in each other's arms. Copulation too can take days, but eventually the male moves on to other pastures. If he is a dominant bear, perhaps on to other females. But the magic doesn't stop there. The fertilized egg (known as a blastocyst) floats around the uterus, waiting to decide whether to affix itself to the uterus wall and become a cub. The deciding factor is whether the female is able to find enough food to put on sufficient fat reserves to support a nursing baby; if she does not, she will simply absorb the blastocyst and try again next year. If she does, she will give birth in January while she is asleep in the den. The newborn cub – blind, hairless and the size of a newborn puppy – will begin its first solo adventure, climbing its way up her body where it will feed on her ready teats.

Humans learned much from and about bears long before we developed the scientific method. In fact, our relationship with grizzly bears stretches back at least 60,000 years. When modern humans left Africa to populate the rest of the planet, *Ursus arctos* was their constant companion. An equally adaptable and omnivorous animal, the brown bear species had already spread across most of southern Eurasia, where it lived in a cold world dominated by ice, tundra and grass.

As the climate warmed and the ice sheets retreated, bears and humans alike moved farther north into Europe and Asia, but the subspecies *Ursus arctos horribilis,* the grizzly bear, always seemed at least one step ahead of us. Grizzly bears would have been better prepared than most to tolerate the harsh conditions found just south of the ice sheets. In fact, grizzly bears recolonized the glacial landscape of central and northern Europe faster than any other carnivorous mammal. Expanding from island refuges bounded by ice in what are now Spain, Italy and Moldova, grizzlies literally followed the southern edge of the ice as it retreated toward the North Pole. Humans soon followed, where we waited together in what is now Siberia for the door to open a passage into the New World.

Grizzly bears beat people into North America by about 30,000 years. The fossil record indicates that grizzlies first crossed into what is now Alaska about 50,000 years ago. The constant ebb and flow of the ice meant that grizzly bears occupied what would become North America in four waves. These first colonists arrived only to be trapped by ice sheets on a tiny island of habitat in what is now Alaska. Isolated and competing against the much bigger short-faced bears and dire wolves, they died out. Nevertheless, as soon as the ice sheets retreated far enough, they returned repeatedly until finally they made their way into North America for good. DNA tests on a jawbone found in an Edmonton,

Alberta gravel pit indicate that grizzlies made it south of the North American ice sheets before the ice had closed off access between Beringia and what is now southern Canada and the continental United States – about 23,000 years ago. By dispersing south, the ancestors of the grizzly bears we now see in Alberta, Montana and Wyoming arrived long before Amerindians.

In many indigenous cultures, the bear is considered the "supreme physician of the woods." Medicine men used a variety of plants, rituals and songs to heal the sick and tend to the wounded. This power and specific herbal remedies were often communicated to the shamans through dreams, at least according to the Lakota. To relieve the symptoms of a cold, the Cheyenne drank tea made from yarrow, which they knew bears ate when they could. Bears also consumed the leaves, berries, stems and roots of kinnikinnick (also known, not surprisingly, as bearberry); something the Crow people must have known as they pulverized its leaves as a remedy for canker sores.

"The bear seems to be a guide for men," wrote Paul Shepard and Barry Sanders in *The Sacred Paw*, their seminal work on the symbolic and spiritual importance of the bear in human consciousness. "We will never know whether men simply discovered that they and it lived parallel lives or, taking note of the bear's example, sought out the same forest resources. But in oral tradition it is said to be the latter." We will never know for sure, and perhaps it doesn't matter. Either way, an intimate relationship formed between humans and what would become known among Amerindians as "Real Bear" and among Europeans as the Great Bear.

Back at the dawn of human consciousness, bears were considered people like us, an idea that may have sparked a revolution in thinking that is still fundamental to our belief systems today. For the antecedents of North America's Indians (and perhaps Europeans too), the bear became an intermediary between this world and the next, and a religious symbol that helped explain the greatest of all life's mysteries.

Consider: Each winter, grizzly bears buried themselves underground as much of the rest of the world "died" beneath the weight of frigid temperatures and a thick blanket of snow. In the spring, often with a cub or two in tow, the bears reappeared along with much of the life our ancestors depended on for their survival: plants, berries, migrating waterfowl, newborn elk and bison.

In many ways, the bear became to Aboriginal cultures what Jesus Christ is to Christians today. It represented not only healing, spring renewal and the idea of rebirth, but the hope of resurrection after the mysterious finality of death. According to Shepard and Sanders, the bear "spoke to the seasons an inescapable analogy to the life of man. Gradually, perhaps over centuries, the human question went beyond How do we survive the cold winter? to How do we survive the cold death? The bear, more than any other teacher, gave an answer to the ultimate question – an astonishing, astounding, improbable answer, enacted rather than revealed."

To think that the grizzly, which evolved alongside the distant ancestors of both Native Americans and Euro-Americans, may have introduced us to the idea of life after death is almost unfathomable today. Yet such a notion may well be so, which seems reason enough to make room in our modern lives for such a remarkable species.

The Death of 56

Bear No. 56 was Banff's version of Jasper National Park's Mary, a tolerant and habituated female grizzly content to raise her cubs in the Bow Valley, near the village of Lake Louise and the Trans-Canada Highway. This was part of her mother's home range, an area she had come to know during the five years she spent following No. 30 through the mountains in search of food. Bear 56 had her first cub during her first winter alone, but as is common for new bear mothers, it quickly vanished into the shadows. In the spring of 2001, at the age of seven, she emerged from the den with two tiny cubs: one male and the other a female.

Although No. 56 and her cubs lived in a national park, they were part of what the

Canadian government classifies as the "north-west grizzly bear population" – a population of some 30,000 individuals that is listed as a "species of special concern." Although this designation affords grizzly bears no legal protection, they are listed as such because their biological characteristics make them particularly sensitive to human activities or natural events.

But grizzly bears, like most "natural resources" in Canada, are managed not by the federal government but by its provincial and territorial counterparts. About half of Canada's grizzlies live in British Columbia, where they are on the "Blue List," BC's version of "special concern." The other half live at low densities north of the 60th parallel, in Nunavut, the Yukon and Northwest Territories. A couple of grizzly bears wandered back into northern Manitoba in 2009 and the government promptly protected them as a species at risk. Bear 56 and her cubs were part of a small population of fewer than 700 grizzlies eking out a tenuous existence in Alberta, where their status is hotly debated.

On the last day of September 2001, a crowd of tourists gathered on the edge of the Bow Valley Parkway just east of Eldon Siding to watch them feed. The trio of bears, feeding on buffaloberries or scavenging train-killed elk within sight of the road, often attracted this kind of attention. Although park officials were concerned that 56 was a little too comfortable around humans, she was also predictable and unthreatening. In any event, she had no choice if she was to make a living in the human-dominated Bow Valley. She was the perfect candidate for a tragic death in Canada's first and most famous national park.

Cruising a buffaloberry patch between the road and the railway, 56 used her nimble, prehensile lips to pluck the ripe fruit. The cubs, high on mother's milk, tumbled and played like puppies. It was too hard to resist, so the tourists stopped in droves to watch what for most of them would be a once-in-a-lifetime experience. Like the scene of an automobile accident, there was an undeniable momentum to the gathering: the more cars that stopped, the more cars pulled over. Soon a bus stopped, too. Numbers made the crowd bolder and people edged closer, all the better to fill the frames of their point-and-shoot cameras with bear. The cubs, inexperienced and unfamiliar with the attention, retreated while mom ate *sans souci*. And then the deep thunder of a locomotive began to move up the valley.

By the time 56 realized what was happening, the noisy train was almost upon them. Her escape route blocked on one side by the watching tourists, Bear 56 panicked and tried to cross the tracks in front of the train. She never made it. The train tossed her dark, limp body toward the watchers, the way a child might toss a teddy bear across a room. For a moment, the struck bear didn't move. Then a scream ripped through the air; a scream that at least one spectator could have sworn was human.

Still for a moment, 56 then struggled to her feet. The train had shattered her femur. She tried to limp away, but her injured leg was unable to bear her weight. As she struggled, shards of bone opened her femoral artery, her life quickly draining from her. The watchers could not believe what they were witnessing. Bear 56 collapsed. All else was still. Only time and the train moved.

The train was long gone by the time Parks Canada wardens arrived to disperse the crowd and collect 56's body. The wardens affixed a transmitter to the male cub's ear and let nature take its course. With no mother to guide and protect them, they would have to make their way on their own. Neither would grow old enough to have cubs of their own.

The death of 56 triggered an avalanche of disquietude from the local community. Bear 56 had been well known and compliant. Like Mary, she had provided locals with numerous glimpses into the life of a grizzly bear sow raising her cubs. Her death was just the latest in a rash of killings. A year earlier, a train near Lake Louise had killed one of 56's two sisters. In May, a subadult male, No. 67, was killed on the highway. In August, the month before 56 died, two of Banff's grizzlies were trapped just outside the park boundary and sent to Lost

Creek, where they were legally shot by Native hunters. In just one year, people killed five of Banff National Park's estimated 60 grizzly bears, three of them females.

It was as if 56's horrific death unleashed the public's frustration at Parks Canada's inability to protect the bears under its charge. Newspaper articles and editorials decried Parks Canada's ineffectiveness and apparent lack of accountability. Less-measured letters to the editor slammed Parks Canada for its apathy and incompetence. Conversations at local coffee shops and pubs criticized the RCMP for not cracking down on speeders, and the Canadian Pacific Railway for irresponsibly baiting bears and other animals to their deaths by leaving tonnes of tempting grain, leaked from freight cars, on the tracks.

Hoping to harness the wave of outrage, I sent out an email inviting anyone who was concerned about the plight of Banff's grizzly bears to meet at my little old miner's house in Canmore. That evening, the living room was packed. There were scientists and teachers, retirees and hiking guides, university professors, veterinarians and massage therapists. Some wore suits and ties, while others wore tie-dye skirts and beads. Some sipped tea, others guzzled beer. The oldest, a retired teacher and notorious social agitator nicknamed Captain Greenshirt, was 65 years old. The youngest, my daughter, Makaila, was just three. Given the diversity of our grassroots effort, almost no one agreed on how to deal with the problem. Some believed education was the only way, while others espoused revolution with a gusto that would have made Che Guevara proud. The more experienced advocates among us, of whom I was not one, suggested a measured and balanced approach. Despite our differences, we all shared one thing in common: to make sure 56 had not died in vain.

Meanwhile, 56's two cubs denned up together for the winter. It seemed an incredible turn of events and raised our hopes that they might survive. But in early June, shortly after they had left their den, the young female was killed by a speeding vehicle in the obligatory but largely ignored and unenforced 70 km/h zone near Lake Louise. The male cub fattened up on berries near Lake Louise and, against all odds, denned up for a second winter. He was clearly a survivor.

For the next two years, our ragtag bunch of idealistic, pissed-off, bear-loving citizens worked tirelessly to implore Parks Canada to improve the situation. The hard work took time away from our families and careers, but it was easy to stay motivated. We felt we had morality on our side, not to mention the strength and clarity of the Canada National Parks Act, which stated that the "maintenance or restoration of ecological integrity...shall be the first priority." We learned there would be a review of Banff National Park's management plan the following year, and we wanted to ensure that the next iteration included a grizzly bear conservation plan. This approach seemed to have worked well in and around Yellowstone National Park, where a well-funded conservation strategy had reduced human-caused grizzly mortality from 2 per cent of the population in the 1970s to less than 0.1 per cent today. At the same time, the approach also succeeded in reducing bear-inflicted injuries of people by 98 per cent.

We were not the only ones sounding the alarm. Bear experts also expressed concern about the excessive death rate of female grizzlies. Males may be bigger and more dominant, but sows are the reproductive future of the species. As the females go, so goes the population. At the time, the 2001 Eastern Slopes Grizzly Bear Project status report stated that "mortality in the adult female cohort is concentrated in Banff National Park. Without the greater survivorship in Kananaskis Country the intrinsic growth rate of the population would probably be negative." Translated, this meant that unprotected areas outside the park were compensating for the unsustainable death toll inside the park. Despite its protected area status, Banff's Bow Valley was becoming a mortality sink.

A small cadre of us coalesced into a board and started coordinating our efforts. We formed an organization, the Bow Valley Grizzly Bear Alliance, and started delegating tasks. Some of us researched grizzly bear biology and the state of the park's bear population. With the help of local biologists, we developed feasible strategies to reduce bear mortalities to sustainable levels. Others designed a website and organized meetings with the public, whom we encouraged to participate in the debate by calling or writing park managers and elected officials. We raised a little money from local foundations to cover the costs, which also allowed us to hire a part-time executive director. In the end, with hopes that it would embarrass Parks Canada into crafting one of their own, we decided to develop our own grizzly bear conservation strategy for Banff National Park.

Meanwhile, the people of Banff and Canmore waited to see if 56's last cub would survive another summer. Only days after exiting the den in the spring, he too succumbed to the absence of a protective mother. Wardens found his body on May 28, 2003, killed by another bear that 56 would have protected him from had she still been alive. Two days later, just north of Lake Louise, near Herbert Lake, a car killed 56's other sister. She left behind a yearling cub, whose fate was never known. In just two years, at least 10 of Banff's 60 grizzly bears, six of them females, had been killed within or near the park boundaries. This staggering number of grizzly deaths exceeded Parks Canada's human-caused mortality rate threshold by 500 per cent.

It was at about this time that I began to burn out. I was working the equivalent of two full-time jobs, one at Y2Y and one on behalf of Banff's bears, while also trying to be a good father and a loving husband. Despite our efforts, nothing seemed to change and the bears kept dying. It was just too much. Stress was beginning to accumulate and the dam holding it back was showing some serious signs of cracking. Something had to change. Although the bears needed our help, I began to feel like it was time to take a break. And then, a grizzly visited me in a dream.

I was walking across a cold and barren hillside, poorly equipped and insufficiently clothed. Snow swirled around me though the ground remained the dun colour of fall. I was worried: worried I wouldn't make it home; worried I wouldn't have enough to eat; worried I would die. A giant bear emerged from the darkness, the white snow swirling around him like smoke. He rose up on his hind legs. "Don't stop," he pleaded. "We need your help. Please don't stop." And then he vanished.

I felt very unsettled when I awoke the next morning. I rarely dream, or at least I don't remember when I do. It seemed crazy that a talking bear visited me in a dream, but it seemed as clear and real as all the other bears I had seen in my life. But what did it mean? Perhaps my subconscious was helping me work through deep-seated conflicts about choices I felt I had to make.

A few days later, I attended a workshop of Native Americans and First Nations people from the Y2Y region. We had invited them to Banff to share their perspectives about what we were trying to do in the region, as well as to find some way to help each other meet any mutual goals. One of the attendees was Levi Holt, a Nez Perce from Idaho. He was a slight man who wore his long black hair in two braids. He didn't speak often, but when he did, his slow, quiet voice resonated with the power of the earth. I told him about my dream.

"Hmmm," he said thoughtfully. "The bears, they are trying to speak to you. They are powerful animals. Perhaps you should listen."

I should not have been surprised that Levi reacted as if talking to bears in dreams was the most natural thing in the world. He told me that Aboriginal myths and stories are full of talking bears. In fact, many Aboriginal creation myths revolve around intimate relationships between grizzly bears and people, often an Aboriginal woman whose half-bear offspring become fierce warriors and tribal leaders. According to Aboriginal cosmology, the appearance of a bear in a dream is a sign that the bear is the dreamer's spirit animal, imbuing the dreamer with the bear's virtuous qualities: ferocity, wisdom, healing.

I did not understand how any of this related to me, but I took the bear dream as a sign that I should stay involved in our grizzly bear conservation efforts. Armed with an increasing amount of information, I began to attend monthly meetings organized by Banff's superintendent to "further dialogue" with the environmental community. Although the meetings were always polite and respectful, little meaningful communication actually took place. We enumerated our grievances, expressed our concerns about how the park was managed, and suggested solutions. Park managers then explained why they could do nothing. We pointed out that many of the measurable goals and objectives in the current management plan were being ignored – the excessive rate of human-caused grizzly bear mortality being one of the most egregious – and that Parks Canada didn't seem to be using "adaptive management" to develop more effective solutions. More often than not, the uniformed bureaucrats on the other side of the table responded with blank stares or shrugged shoulders. Having spoken off the record to many Parks Canada staff, I knew that many of them also believed there was a problem.

One day my frustration got the better of me. "Listen," I said, looking acting Banff superintendent Jillian Roulet in the eye, "If I were to develop a five-year work plan at my place of employment and I failed to meet my goals and objectives every year for five years, I would get fired." Then I slammed my hand down on the table. I wish I could say it was for effect, but it was simply an involuntary reflex; a manifestation of how frustrating it was to try to influence the direction of a bureaucracy so betrothed to the status quo that it makes a supertanker in high seas seem nimble by comparison. "If you're not going to do anything to meet the 1 per cent mortality target you committed to, then why don't you just change it?"

There was no response and the meeting ended shortly thereafter. Then the superintendent stopped calling and the meetings disappeared altogether.

Undeterred, and to a chorus of local support and media attention, we released "The Bear Necessities: A Grizzly Bear Conservation Strategy for Banff National Park" on the eve of the 2003 management plan review. "The Bear Necessities" was predicated on the idea that Banff and the other Rocky Mountain national parks should become the heart of grizzly bear conservation in the southern Canadian Rocky Mountains. While most of the surrounding landscape is overseen by the provincial governments of Alberta and BC, which are more concerned with exploiting Canada's natural resources than protecting them, Parks Canada's legal mandate obliges it to ensure that grizzly bear populations not only *survive* but also *thrive*. We hoped to turn our national parks into models of responsible management that produce enough grizzly bears to enthrall tourists and buoy up flagging populations outside their protective boundaries.

The nuts and bolts of the plan were fairly simple. A major source of bear mortality is the highway, so fence it all the way to the BC border and build crossing structures to encourage wildlife movement. Then restrict human use north of Lake Louise, the only one of the three important grizzly bear areas that is overrun by profiteers and tourists. In addition, clamp down on speeders, who endanger bears and people alike on the roads in Banff. Deal with another major source of mortality by slowing trains to a crawl and forcing the CPR to eradicate the egregious amounts of grain spilled on the tracks each year. Finally, enact temporary closures in other parts of the park that bears use heavily during certain seasons.

There was pushback, of course, which we expected. Led by the pro-business Association for Mountain Parks Protection & Enjoyment, Banff's billion-dollar business community opposed even the notion of curtailing human use of any part of the park at any time of the year. "Parks are for people too" was their mantra. While they also purport to support wildlife protection, there was only room for grizzly bears and billy goats if they could eke out an existence on whatever territory we hadn't turned into roads, ski resorts, golf courses or the hotels, motels, restaurants and other man-made "attractions" that service two million well-paying visitors each year.

Despite the deep pockets of Banff's well-paid lobbyists, we seemed to be making headway. Articles appeared in all major newspapers and television crews descended on Banff to cover the story. Tracey Henderson, a local vet and our part-time staffer, was invited to speak on various radio programs, including CBC's *Wild Rose Country*. The word got out and our website hummed as hundreds of people sent letters to Parks Canada, voicing their concern and asking that our solution be included in the revised management plan. It looked like we might just win the day.

When the smoke finally cleared and the final version of the Banff management plan was approved by Parliament in 2004, we discovered that our conservation strategy had made the cut. Only it wasn't really a "strategy" at all, at least not in any real sense of the word. Instead, it was a "Strategic Framework for the

Conservation of Grizzly Bears in Banff National Park," a wishy-washy rag cleverly constructed by policy wonks in Ottawa to say everything and nothing at all. The strategic goal, "to contribute to the long-term persistence of a healthy population of grizzly bears," was immeasurably weak. The objectives and "key actions" were peppered with wiggle words like "minimize," "emphasize" and "demonstrate." There were no details about how they might "provid[e] for the security" of subadult and adult females while "emphasiz[ing] decreas[ed] human-caused mortality." Nor was there any information about how to "reduce the frequency of human–grizzly bear interactions." The only meaningful target was to maintain the current but unmet goal of "reducing the number of grizzly bears killed as a result of human activity to less than 1 per cent of the population annually." Yet, there was no firm commitment even to this. Instead, they obligated themselves only to "strive" to reduce the number of grizzly bears killed, as if the striving itself would keep grizzly bears alive and the law obeyed.

There was reason to hope, however. Parks Canada has done the right thing in the past. For instance, after a series of gruesome maulings near the town of Banff in 1980, Parks Canada shut down the garbage dump near Lake Louise and installed bear-proof garbage bins in the national parks. This essentially halved the number of human-caused mortalities in the Rocky Mountain national parks: from an average of 4.9 per year in the 1980s to 2.2 during the 1990s. After the 1993 Banff–Bow Valley Study recognized that development was rending the ecological fabric of Banff National Park into an unrecognizable simulacrum of its former self – like a fine Persian carpet cut into a million tiny pieces – Parks Canada stood up to the business lobby and began making reparations. Under the leadership of then federal Minister of Canadian Heritage Sheila Copps, a cap was placed on development in the Banff townsite. Parks Canada's horse stable and a scout camp were both removed to facilitate wildlife movement in the Bow Valley. Commitments were made to continue fencing the

Trans-Canada Highway, which some wardens had taken to calling The Meatmaker. Under the right leadership, it seemed, the striving, the minimizing, the emphasizing and the demonstrating just might lead to positive change and a whole lot fewer dead bears. Only time would tell.

And so, we moved on to other things. The Bow Valley Grizzly Bear Alliance morphed into the Grizzly Bear Alliance, and we began working to protect grizzly bears outside of the national parks. Alberta's beleaguered grizzly bear population was worse off than Banff's, and the provincial government, which ostensibly looked after it, made George Bush's environmental policies look progressive. There was plenty to do.

Meanwhile, protected by the strength of the Canada National Parks Act and the ostentatious-sounding "Strategic Framework for the Conservation of Grizzly Bears in Banff National Park," Banff's grizzly bears continued to die in record numbers. In 2004, the year the Banff management plan was amended, three sows died – one on the highway and two of natural causes – leaving six cubs orphaned.

The worst year of all was 2005. A 1-year-old female was killed on the train tracks near Castle Junction. Then a well-known female, No. 66, was killed on the tracks not far from the Banff townsite. Her three 1-year-old cubs survived, but within a month, two of them had been killed on the highway and one was captured by Parks Canada officials and sent to a zoo. The most tragic story took place in my hometown. That summer, one of No. 30's orphaned cubs, now 4 years old, wandered out of the park and into the town of Canmore. Three runners encountered him on a trail above the Silver Tip Golf Course. While two of them left the area immediately, the third, my friend Isabelle Dubé, decided to climb a tree. When a provincial conservation officer arrived to help, he found No. 99 crouched over Isabelle's lifeless body and shot him dead.

Despite the fact that grizzly bears have been a Parks Canada management priority for 10 years, the story isn't a whole lot different today than it was when 56 lost her race against the train in 2001. Importantly, it is not only grizzly bears; they are simply indicators of a wider problem. Banff's roads and railways, despite fences and overpasses, constantly kill wolves. Moose, historically much more abundant, are more or less absent from the eastern Bow Valley. At the western end of Banff, more than a dozen moose are killed on highways each year. Parks Canada stood by for 25 years while human activity reduced Banff's only caribou herd from 25 to just four individuals, despite their protection under Canada's Species at Risk Act. In April 2009, the rest of the herd disappeared forever beneath the thick snow of a spring avalanche.

Black bears too are dying, at nearly twice the rate of grizzlies. Parks Canada has no idea how this is affecting the black bear population, because they've never bothered to figure out how many there are. In 2009, Sid Marty, a former Banff warden who left Parks Canada in disgust to pursue a career as a writer, said, "The idea that we are somehow protecting these bears efficiently is nonsense. It seems that an attitude of indifference to the smaller species of bear continues to be as prevalent at Parks Canada headquarters today as it was in earlier decades. Obviously, we still have a long way to go."

The Banff management plan is up for review again, and the 2008 "State of the Park" report that kicked it off is enlightening. Overall, the report echoes the conclusions of its predecessors over the last 15 years. Terrestrial ecosystems are in decline. The grizzly bear population is in poor condition, largely because the current human-caused mortality target has been exceeded for the last 10 years, sometimes by more than 500 per cent. Parks Canada remains "concerned" that this leaves the population "susceptible to decline." With so much room for improvement, I felt hopeful that Parks Canada would finally deliver a beefed-up management plan, with a hefty budget, that would prevent grizzlies and other animals from being slaughtered like cattle in our most famous national park.

The draft version of the revised management plan, sent out for review in late 2009, could not

have been more disappointing. Banff's grizzlies are part of a small population of Alberta
bears recommended to be listed as a threatened
species. While there may be some genetic ex-
change across the Continental Divide into BC,
the rugged terrain and busy highways have
left the Clearwater subpopulation (of which
Banff's bears are a part) increasingly isolated.
A recent population study, one of the best of
its kind in the world, found approximately
100 bears in this subpopulation. Most of these
bears spend some portion of their lives in
Banff National Park. Beleaguered by highways,
industrial tourism and, outside the park, urban
sprawl, oil and gas development, logging and
rapacious levels of motorized recreation, this
small population is almost surely declining.
Unless we curtail human activities and reduce
bear mortality, the risk that this population
will follow Banff's caribou into oblivion will
only increase.

What was Parks Canada's response to this
crisis? According to the draft management plan,
Banff's goal is to work with British Columbia

and Alberta to maintain "a non-declining" grizzly bear population in the Rocky Mountains. This is a low bar for a bureaucracy that Parks Canada CEO Alan Latourelle recently heralded as a "world leader" in recovering species at risk. Committing to maintain the status quo of a grizzly bear population that is threatened with extirpation is hardly the kind of leadership one expects from Canada's national parks. In fact, it is the opposite of leadership; it is a cowardly abdication of its legal obligation to protect Canada's incredible natural heritage.

For once, Parks Canada took my advice. Rather than strengthen the management plan to eliminate the sources of excessive human-caused grizzly bear mortality, Parks Canada simply weakened the allowable mortality threshold. Unable to meet its own human-caused mortality target of no more than 1 per cent of the population, the draft management plan essentially removed any limits on the number of grizzlies that could die in Canada's renowned national park. It is now okay for one female grizzly to be killed each year, up from one female every three years in the old management plan. There is no mention of a mortality threshold for males, which one presumes could die by the busload without the bureaucrats in Ottawa so much as raising a collective eyebrow.

Is "one" the kind of conservative, precautionary number one might expect of Parks Canada? No. There are approximately 60 grizzly bears in Banff National Park itself. The almost universally accepted human-caused mortality limit for grizzly bears in this part of the world is less than 4 per cent of the population each year, with no more than 1.2 per cent being females. That means that in Banff National Park, an average of fewer than 0.72 females and 1.68 males can die from human causes each year if we are to maintain the population. That's about four females and seven males every six years. The new management plan proposes to allow six females and an indeterminate number of males over the same period. Parks Canada has chosen a bar so low that even a even a snake could slither over it.

Habitat security for grizzly bears, like mortality targets, remains unmet. Grizzly bear habitat is secure when bears can forage with little human-caused disturbance. This is important because it allows them to get the nutrition they need without getting habituated or killed. The purported targets for habitat security in the draft revision of the management plan are "78 per cent of grizzly bear habitat," which is a science-based and reasonable target. After all, the current target in Montana's Northern Continental Divide Ecosystem, where grizzlies are recovering rather successfully under the protections afforded by the us Endangered Species Act, is only 68 per cent. It would seem that 78 per cent is the kind of target appropriate for a national park, the first priority of which is to maintain or restore ecological integrity by protecting natural resources and natural processes.

Then you read the fine print. The target, it seems, does not apply to the entire park. Instead, only "21 of 27 landscape units" need to meet this criterion. As much as 25 per cent of

Banff National Park is not required to meet any habitat security targets at all. Today, only 15 landscape units satisfy the 78 per cent target and the habitat around Lake Louise, where most of Banff's grizzlies die, is only 7 per cent secure. A 2002 study found that Banff and the other Rocky Mountain national parks (Jasper, Kootenay and Yoho) boasted only 43 per cent secure habitat. Banff, being the most developed of the three, is likely lower than that. Yellowstone National Park, by comparison, boasts 86 per cent habitat security, which is why it has such low numbers of grizzly bear deaths and bear-inflicted injuries. Once again, Parks Canada has set another very low bar, one that almost guarantees the carnage will continue.

Although the deadline for public input had long since passed, the implications of these revisions for grizzly bears seemed rather significant. So, I decided to email my thoughts on the matter to Banff superintendent Kevin van Tighem. To my surprise, he responded immediately with a kind note suggesting we meet.

Two days later, we were sitting across from each other at a coffee shop in Banff.

Van Tighem is a career bureaucrat and fellow writer who has worked in several national parks in Western Canada. He has also proved to be a fierce defender of the environment, writing passionately about environmental issues and even actively organizing against harmful industrial projects, such as the illegal construction of Alberta's Oldman River dam. He would seem the perfect choice to safeguard Banff's precious natural resources, but ever since he took the reins in Banff, some insiders worry that he had "drunk the visitor experience Kool-Aid" being served up in Ottawa. After a few minutes of small talk, I asked what he thought about my concerns.

"I'd argue that we *are* making ecological integrity the first priority as defined by the National Parks Act," he said. He concurred that ecological integrity *was* the priority when considering management decisions, but only in the context of educating and entertaining visitors, which were also part of Parks Canada's mission.

With respect to bears, he said, "We've dealt with all the low-hanging fruit. Now we're left with the more difficult problems. Now we're worrying about one female every year or two. That's a lot less than we used to [worry about]."

I was somewhat surprised at his rather favourable interpretation of the situation. For one thing, he narrowly defines Parks Canada's mandate in a way that didn't seem to make ecological integrity a priority at all. He also underestimates the number of grizzlies that are being killed, which even the 2008 State of the Parks report that he approved identifies as a major problem. And he didn't even mention the fact that Parks Canada hasn't met its own mortality or habitat security targets for more than a decade.

Shaun Fluker, a law professor at the University of Calgary, doesn't share van Tighem's optimism. In a recently published journal article, "Ecological Integrity in Canada's National Parks: The False Promise of Law," Fluker concludes that despite a strengthening of the national parks legislation in 1988 and 2001 to prioritize environmental protection, both Parks Canada and the federal court have "read down the priority of the ecological integrity first priority as simply a factor to be taken into account in parks decision-making. Not only is the preservation of nature not the first priority in the national parks, it isn't even a presumption in parks decision-making."

Meanwhile, for the first time in the history of national park management, Parks Canada decided to include in the revised management plan an obligation to increase tourism. Not content to leave marketing efforts to the businesses, lobby groups, tourism boards and provincial governments who have branded Banff as "Canada's protected playground," Parks Canada has now committed itself to increase visitation by 2 per cent a year. This is a fundamental shift in policy that hearkens back to the founding of Banff in 1885, when both the Canadian Pacific Railway and the Canadian government eyed the newly discovered hot springs with lascivious greed. "Since we can't export the scenery," said American railroader and CPR vice-president Sir William Cornelius Van Horne, "we shall have to import the tourists." Chief CPR engineer Sir Sandford Fleming noted that tourists "would become a source of general profit."

The move to increase visitation is based on a false assumption that has been handed down by Ottawa to be flogged by the very people who should know better. Greg Fenton, superintendent of Jasper National Park, recently stated that the "very future of the parks depends on getting more people to actually visit and appreciate them."

The claim is ridiculous. There is no question that we need a shift in consciousness to create a better, more respectful relationship with the natural world. We do need natural places that provide people with positive experiences. However, national parks are supposed to offer the pre-eminent level of protection to a natural world under assault everywhere. Many of the most popular parks are already underfunded and overused, their primary mandate to protect nature undermined by government indifference. Development, especially the infrastructure required to facilitate the industrial-scale tourism seen in Banff, can be as harmful to ecological integrity as strip mines and clear-cuts. Increasing this kind of visitation places a burden on our national parks that they simply cannot bear.

The very reason we have parks and protected areas is because too many people are doing too much everywhere else. That is why Parliament, in 1988 and 2001, made ecological integrity the first priority. If we do not protect what is left of the natural world from our insidious industriousness, we will lose, in the words of Canada's first commissioner of national parks, James Harkin, "the very thing that distinguishes [our national parks] from the outside world." Increasingly, grizzly bears have come to symbolize the very health of our ecosystems, which supply all of us with trillions of dollars worth of ecological "services" that we cannot hope to recreate if we destroy them. If we cannot protect grizzly bears (and caribou and wolves) in our national parks, then where can we protect them?

Besides, Banff and the rest of Canada's national parks are not relevant to Canadians because they provide business and recreational opportunities; there are plenty of other places to invest money and golf 18 holes. National parks are "for people" because they help to fulfill our national and international commitments to protect biodiversity. They also help to fill our souls with the primal need to connect with nature *on its own terms*. Indeed, they can also provide business and recreational opportunities, but only to those willing to experience nature without destroying it.

It is almost impossible to imagine how Parks Canada might reach the human-caused grizzly mortality and habitat security targets that it has not been able to meet so far while at the same time allowing the addition of ziplines, mountain biking and summer use at the ski hills. While visitors should certainly be able to enjoy our national parks, it is Parks Canada's legal obligation to ensure we do not love them to death with our industrial-strength affection. There is already too much human activity in

Banff National Park, and more will only erode the park's ecological integrity further.

That's the bad news. The good news, ironically, is that although Parks Canada keeps itself very busy, it clearly has a hard time achieving the goals it sets for itself. So, it's unlikely that it will be able to increase visitation any time soon.

Success South of the Border

Americans love to wrap themselves in mythology and the symbols they have adopted for themselves. Consider the bald eagle or the Stars and Stripes, which have become iconic symbols of freedom, independence and the United States of America. Whether Americans are more or less free and independent than other people does not really matter; this is how they choose to see and represent themselves to the world.

The residents of Missoula, Montana, chose the grizzly bear as their symbol, and in true American fashion, they have honoured it big time. In fact, there is little doubt that Missoula has a greater density of grizzly bears than anywhere else in the contiguous United States. As the University of Montana mascot, grizzlies are on flags, T-shirts and posters wherever you look. The football field is called Washington-Grizzly Stadium, and the university swimming pool bears the Grizzly name too. Grizzly prints embed the sidewalks as if fossilized dinosaur tracks. Bronze statues greet you on campus and along the river trail, the latter a larger-than-life demon whose face is twisted into a ferocious snarl.

More than a dozen life-sized fibreglass grizzly statues inhabit local storefronts, building foyers and truck stops, each garbed in the unique vision of a local artist. Each of these statues was painted as part of a fundraiser for the college football team. One bears on its side the scene of a fly-fisherman angling for trout and another the bright-red bodies of spawning salmon. Others allow us to peer inside the grizzly: "Bare Bones" showing off its skeleton and "Heart Felt Bear" offering a window to what lies inside. There are writing themes and landscape themes, postmodern themes and pop culture themes. One carries the football team to greater heights, another the stars at night.

Businesses too bear the grizzly's name. There's a Grizzly Grocer. Grizzly Property Management rents apartments and Grizzly Liquor sells Grizzly Beer. You can buy shrubs at the Pink Grizzly Nursery and coffee at the Grizzly Bean. You can even have your bikini line waxed at Grizzly Bare. The Great Bears are everywhere.

Perhaps more significantly, the real things recently have returned to the Rattlesnake Wilderness on the edge of town. It is difficult to know which came first, the resurgence of the real bears on Missoula's periphery or its obsession with the mythical ones that line its streets. Perhaps it doesn't matter. Missoula is the Grizzly City.

I knew none of this, of course, when I decided to quit my job at Y2Y and move to Missoula to work on a master's degree and a book about the disappearance of the Great Plains grizzly bear. It was nice to live in a place where grizzly bears were such an important part of everyday life. My own growing obsession with these mythical beasts had provided a touchstone, a guide in a busy and alienating world. Alberta, my home, is a pragmatic magnet for engineers and accountants intent on transforming all of our native grasslands, foothills and forests into profitable natural resources like timber, coal, natural gas and oil – no matter the cost.

In a sense, it is a real-life example of what Theodor Seuss Geisel (a.k.a. Dr. Seuss) warned us about when he published *The Lorax* in 1971, the very year I moved to Alberta. *The Lorax* is a parody of unrelenting industrialization rationalized away as the provision of "things everybody needs," even as the water is poisoned and the air defiled, driving the bears, fish and birds to extinction and the humans elsewhere. I doubt Dr. Seuss had ever been to Alberta, but he could not have been more prescient about its future. It would be an uproariously funny book if it were not proving to be so true.

I was delighted to learn that the US Grizzly Bear Recovery Program office was located on the Missoula campus, just a two-minute walk from my office. Chris Servheen, the man who had overseen grizzly bear recovery in the lower

48 states for most of the last 30 years, would be happy to sit on my thesis committee.

The ongoing recovery of grizzly bears in the contiguous United States is one of the most politically contentious recovery efforts ever undertaken anywhere. This is in large part because grizzly bears require a lot of real estate but have no money to pay for it. Unlike the Banff springs snail, an endangered species found only in a few small thermal pools in Banff National Park, maintaining wild grizzly bear populations on the landscape precludes a whole lot of recreational and industrial activity. To keep the Banff springs snail alive means prohibiting drunken teenagers from sneaking into the hot pools late at night. To keep grizzlies alive means limiting mining, ranching, oil and gas wells, roads, hunting, logging, poaching and a slew of other human activities that directly and indirectly result in dead bears. Also, people living and working in bear habitat must take precautionary measures, some of which are time consuming and expensive. The resulting increase in government oversight doesn't always sit well with people who still live by the myth of the frontier that suggests that everyone can do everything everywhere all the time. And so the acrimony grew.

When restrictions on motorized vehicle use came into force in the early 1990s, some ATV users refused to obey the new rules. Servheen refers to these people as "knuckleheads." They cut the locks off gates and exercised their perceived right to use the roads and trails they had always used. In response, the US government sent in law enforcement officials to lay charges and hand out fines. Eventually they began confiscating the quads and dirt bikes of the most recidivist perpetrators, slinging their machines up out of the forest with helicopters and leaving the rideless yahoos to hump it home on foot.

This, of course, did not enhance the popularity of the grizzly bear recovery coordinator or the environmentalists that used the law to staunchly defend the grizzly bear. Servheen began getting hate mail and threatening phone calls. Public meetings often saw slanderous tirades, and personal insults were thrown every which way. Threats of violence were also not unheard of, as more than a few environmental advocates working in rural locales tell of vandalism and bullet holes in their walls.

If you think this kind of abuse made Servheen and the environmental movement allies, think again. All along the way, many (but not all) environmentalists believed Servheen and the US Fish & Wildlife Service were not doing enough to protect the grizzly bears. Environmentalists routinely threw jabs and hooks in the media. They also filed lawsuit after lawsuit against various government departments for not obeying laws and policies meant to protect grizzly bears. While the lawsuits seem justified, as the environmentalists won most of them, the acrimony that accumulated over the years has left a sour taste in the mouths of many key players.

Servheen has accused Louisa Willcox in particular of taking personal shots at him and even of trying to get him fired. She maintains she has no beef with Servheen in particular, but, like an aggressive sow protecting her cubs, she continues to defend the Yellowstone grizzly population. The US Fish & Wildlife Service is trying to remove grizzlies from the protections of the Endangered Species Act (ESA). While Servheen feels the ESA has sufficiently recovered the Yellowstone population, Willcox has led the charge to prevent delisting. She and various litigious environmental groups cite concerns over the security of important food sources that may worsen as the climate warms.

Still, it seems like these two opponents, working together in symbiotic opposition – her yoga-inspired yin and his boot-wearing yang – seem to have gotten the job done. While the story in Banff makes it seem impossible to share a busy national park with grizzlies, the American experience indicates it can be done. The Yellowstone grizzly bear population is on the verge of being delisted and Servheen believes the population in the Northern Continental Divide Ecosystem (NCDE) could follow suit in as little as five years. The NCDE lies just south of the Canadian border and shares a population of more than 1000 grizzly bears with British Columbia and Alberta. In Montana, this population has rebounded with such vigour that grizzly bears have been found as far east as Fort Benton, recolonizing parts of the Great Plains where they haven't been seen in 125 years. At a time when four species *every hour* are becoming extinct, this is an incredible story of restraint and responsibility.

When I asked Servheen what the keys to success have been, he mentioned education, good people, political support and healthy budgets. "What about the Endangered Species Act? Could you have done it without the ESA?"

"No," he says. "No way. Without the ESA, we wouldn't have been able to recover grizzlies."

I know he would like to say otherwise. I know he would like to say that Americans in the Greater Yellowstone Ecosystem just decided what needed to be done and then worked together to make it happen. But the reality is that there wouldn't be 600 grizzly bears in Greater Yellowstone without the authority to enforce the ESA and force local and state governments to change the way they do business.

More importantly, grizzly recovery has also relied on the ability of American citizens to use the courts to ensure the federal government obeys its own laws. Without these two forces, there might be 250 grizzlies in Yellowstone National Park but the population would never be big enough to be called "recovered" and success would always be just over the horizon.

Servheen, the only person in the world to oversee the successful recovery of a grizzly bear population, had been invited to Alberta to advise the government on grizzly bear management north of the 49th parallel. So, I asked him to compare what he found in Alberta with what he was used to at home. He was quiet for a moment, and then he said: "Alberta reminds me of the United States in the 1950s, before we had strong environmental legislation. When we still believed there were no limits."

Before I left Montana with a master's degree and a half-finished book under my arm, my daughter and I made one last trip to Yellowstone. She lived in Washington, DC, with her mother now, and it had been years since she had seen Yellowstone's bears and wolves. We only had one day, so we spent it driving to all the best places to look for grizzlies. It was the middle of summer and the roads were hot and crowded. Normally I make a point of avoiding Yellowstone at this time of year. I prefer to arrive, as I had when Willcox brought me down for the first time, with the songbirds in the spring. At that time, the tourists are still at work in their office towers and the last of the winter snow keeps the animals in the valley bottoms, where they're easy to spot from the road. Unlike in Banff, Yellowstone staff encourage people to stop along roadsides and watch the park's wildlife. In late May or early June, Yellowstone is a real-life version of the Discovery Channel.

Today, the grizzlies, all 600 of them, were hiding. We spent the morning in the Lamar Valley, where we saw some wolves and plenty of bison and elk. After grabbing an ice cream cone in Mammoth, we made a dash down to visit Old Faithful geyser, which faithfully gushed into the sky shortly after we arrived.

Still, there was no sign of bears and it was time to start for home.

Not far from Hayden Valley, in the dusky light of early evening, a chestnut-coloured griz crept up over the sun-scorched hill to our left. "Look, daddy!" Makaila shouted, barely able to contain herself as she pointed through the windshield. "Cubs! Two of them!"

It was a sow and two tiny cubs, which, I couldn't help but think, were about the same age as 56's the day she died under the wheels of that cursed train. These cubs wouldn't have to contend with railways or high-speed highways. When they do finally die, probably a decade or more on, they would at least have the dignity of dying a natural death. In the early 21st century, that is the biggest gift we can give a grizzly bear.

The Alberta Disadvantage

By the time I returned to Canada in 2008, the Grizzly Bear Alliance (GBA) had folded and Alberta's grizzly bear population was in deepening trouble. GBA's board members and underpaid staff of one had burned out; there was little energy and no money left to do much of anything. I was too busy writing to resurrect the GBA, so the fight would have to be carried by other groups and individuals who have been working to protect Alberta's grizzly bear: the Alberta Wilderness Association, Canadian Parks & Wilderness Society, Yellowstone to Yukon Conservation Initiative and, more recently, Louisa Willcox's Natural Resources Defense Council (NRDC) from the United States.

One of these individuals is an aging environmental warrior named Jim Pissot, who has been fighting to protect wildlife and wilderness since the end of the Vietnam war 35 years ago. Pissot, who lives in Canmore, Alberta, with his wife Valerie, is not your stereotypical environmentalist. He is a Yale graduate and former machinist who is as comfortable rebuilding the engine in his '48 Chevy as he is conversing about Italian architecture and Nietzsche's philosophy. But what he loves most is wild nature. While most people his age are planning for retirement, this avuncular 62-year-old spends his days decapitating invasive thistles with a hand-held scythe or standing in front of Calgary's Palliser Hotel in a bear costume, handing out pamphlets about CP Rail's dismal record of killing grizzlies in Banff (as the company's AGM reports its profits inside the hotel).

Born to a Canadian mother and an American father, Pissot grew up in Utah, where he became a key figure in securing the federal Utah Wilderness Act of 1984. He returned to university in his early thirties to complete an undergraduate degree and then, after scoring in the 99th percentile on the GRE (the mandatory entrance exam for graduate studies in the US), he chose Yale. In the 25 years since, however, Pissot has learned the hard way what it means to fight tooth and nail for wildlife species bound for oblivion. Battling to save the endangered northern spotted owl in the Pacific Northwest in the early 1990s, he toiled 15-hour days for the National Audubon Society, mapping owl habitat and building local support in Washington State, where the timber industry was clear-cutting the last vestiges of old-growth forest that still harboured a shrinking spotted owl population. Ultimately, Pissot and his colleagues prevailed with lawsuits against the federal government. But the Owl Wars, as they became known, were contentious, hard fought and even dangerous: there were days when he feared for his life and the safety of his family.

After a successful stint as a senior vice-president for the National Parks Conservation Association in Washington, DC, Pissot migrated north to Alberta to head up the Y2Y initiative, which is where I met him. Surprisingly, Pissot says his work north of the Medicine Line has proven much more difficult – albeit somewhat safer – than in the US, where "we have the full power of the Endangered Species Act and the citizen's right to sue government to obey its own laws. In Canada, federal legislation to protect endangered species is weak and the provincial laws are even weaker. And there is literally no way to force either government to obey their own laws. It's like fighting with one hand tied behind your back." Still, he fights, in part because of his love for wild nature, in part because he cannot abide the arrogant disregard Canadian governments seem to have for both the democratic process and the natural resources they have been charged to protect.

It is all but impossible not to agree with him. Research I conducted for a graduate paper comparing environmental governance made it startlingly clear that Canada's record was not only worse than that of the United States, it was one of the worst in the developed world. While I had always believed Canada was a "world leader" in all things environmental, I was beginning to see that this, like Americans' love of independence and freedom, is simply a myth we Canadians like to cling to and project to the world.

When asked to write a magazine article about Alberta's track record protecting species at risk, I decided to shadow Pissot while he gave a presentation at a sold-out workshop on grizzly bear research and management in Alberta. Pissot was one of seven guest speakers that included biologists, hunters and bureaucrats. After a brief introduction, Pissot rested his hands on the lectern and stared out at the crowd. With his spectacles, blue blazer and balding pate rimmed with grey hair, Pissot looked every bit the college professor he could have been had he not dedicated himself to advocating on behalf of the world's endangered species. The giant screen behind him illuminated his raison d'être: "Path to Extinction or Path to Recovery? The Mismanagement of Alberta's Endangered Grizzly Bear."

In the audience with me were some 200 foresters, biologists, bureaucrats, oil and gas workers, hunters, environmentalists and off-road vehicle enthusiasts – most of them lukewarm or outright hostile to what he had to say. Pissot began with the simple logic of a Far Side cartoon, which elicited a smattering of quiet laughter from the crowd. Two giant bears stood tall at the mouth of a cave, beating back an onslaught of Neanderthals wielding lumpy clubs. "Criminy," the caption read, "every summer there are more and more of these things."

The caricature is remarkably appropriate. In the 1980s, government biologists in Alberta became concerned that the industrialization of grizzly bear habitat and a generous sport hunt were impacting the health of the bear population. The hunt was restricted in 1988, and in 1990 a grizzly bear management plan was developed and adopted to prevent the grizzly population from declining. The plan recognized that grizzly bear habitat in Alberta was in a sorry state and deteriorating rapidly, and that the population, then estimated to be 800 animals, needed to be increased to at least 1000 to prevent a crisis. Even then, the management plan recognized that the fate of Alberta's grizzly bear population would depend on maintaining and restoring the health of Alberta's wildlands.

Fast forward to 2002 – a year in which at least 35 grizzlies were poached, shot by licensed hunters or killed in vehicle collisions – and not much had changed. A status report released by the government claimed that the same forces that had prompted concern in 1990 were still at play and putting the province's grizzly bear population at risk: excessive mortality, small population size and increasingly fragmented and developed habitat. Incredibly, the status report also claimed that despite these worrying trends, the Alberta grizzly bear population actually had *increased* to more than 1000 animals, just as the management plan had suggested. The government, it seemed, was right on track, and it had barely changed a thing.

The government's optimism, however, was not shared by Alberta's Endangered Species Conservation Committee (AESCC), which came to a slightly different conclusion in 2002. A government-appointed committee that includes representatives from the hunting community, industry, academia and government, the AESCC repeated the concerns laid out in the 1990 management plan and the 2002 status report. However, rather than celebrate a population increase, it recommended that the Alberta grizzly bear be listed as a threatened species. With fewer than 1,000 bears left in the province, it was time, agreed the AESCC, to get serious about recovering a species that was clearly in trouble.

The government wasn't so sure and it refused to accept the recommendation. Then, in 2004, a government-commissioned analysis by University of Alberta biologist Mark Boyce found that the government's assessment of a population increase between 1990 and 2002 was unwarranted. It seems that despite the fact other jurisdictions – namely the US government, in Yellowstone – had invested the time and money required to get reasonably accurate estimates, the Alberta government chose to use a "made-in-Alberta" methodology that involved "questionable practices" which "are not scientifically defensible" and which potentially led to predictions that were "not biologically possible."

In response, the government began a $3-million bear population study that it hoped would exculpate them by confirming, once and for all, that there were more than 1000 grizzly bears in Alberta. To its consternation, the results only highlighted the urgency of the problem, revealing that in reality only about 700 grizzlies remained in the protected areas and remnant wilderness on the western fringe of the province. In the same period that the grizzly population in Yellowstone had tripled, Alberta's population remained precariously small.

Yet, eight years after the AESCC's recommendation, protecting the grizzly bear as a threatened species and making meaningful changes to the way grizzly bear habitat is managed haven't even begun. To its credit, the Alberta government did suspend the grizzly bear hunt. And it did convene a grizzly bear recovery team to draft a recovery plan (for a species it has so far refused to admit is in need of recovery), but the plan is extremely weak and there is no money in the budget to implement it anyway.

The weakness of the recovery plan is a testament to the "multi-stakeholder" nature of the planning process. The government handpicked a group of people from a variety of "sectors" to help draft the recovery plan. Some environmentalists and bear biologists were on the team, including Mark Boyce from the University of Alberta, Robert Barclay from the University of Calgary, Mike Gibeau from Parks Canada and Gord Stenhouse from the Foothills Research Institute, which conducts grizzly bear research on behalf of the government. Most of the participants, however, were from government or industry, which stood to lose the most if the government had to implement protections for grizzly bears. But according to Boyce, it wasn't only the industry reps who proved resistant to change:

> The government representatives were as difficult as the industry people. Even the government people were representatives from Energy, Public Lands and Forestry. They were not biologists with a conservation

agenda; they were there to try to protect the paradigm that Alberta is open to business.

"As we all know, it is the rapidly deteriorating landscape conditions influenced by industrial development that is spelling doom for Alberta's grizzly bears," Boyce told me in an email. "And the province has already decided to let them go. Terminate the hunt, list the species as threatened, provide no funding for research or monitoring, and let them quietly disappear from most of Alberta while we continue to provide oil and gas for our fuel-hungry diets."

The biggest bone of contention, of course, was roads. The oil, gas and forestry industries, and the provincial government that encourages them, do not want limits placed on where and how industry can access these resources. While everyone on the recovery team eventually came around to understand that limiting human access was the key to grizzly bear persistence, not everyone agreed on how it should be accomplished.

The US experience indicates that even with strong regulations and adequate enforcement, managing public access once roads have been built just doesn't work. Keeping the recovery zone relatively road free (no more than 0.6 kilometres per square kilometre) was the only strategy that worked.

"I'm worried about the degradation of habitat due to roads and industrial development," said Boyce, an American biologist who was involved in the US recovery process earlier in his career. "Roads and bears don't mix."

In Alberta, however, such thoughts are tantamount to heresy. In 2006, when Gord Stenhouse, the Alberta government's former grizzly bear biologist, told CBC news that roads were a problem for grizzly bears, he was removed from his position. At first, government officials tried to deny that Stenhouse was the government's grizzly bear biologist, but when journalists discovered that his business cards and the government website indicated that he indeed *was* the province's grizzly bear biologist, the government changed its tune. Instead, government officials maintained he had simply been "seconded" to the Foothills Model Forest (now the Foothills Research Institute) to oversee the province's grizzly bear research from there. But the message was clear: roads are here to stay and no one in government better say otherwise.

As then Minister of Sustainable Development Mike Cardinal said in the same CBC report, closing roads or limiting access might "have a very negative impact on the overall economy in Alberta.... We're used to a certain type of lifestyle in Alberta. It costs about $20-billion a year to run it in the province. We have to keep developing our resources because resources have to be developed."

Instead, industry and government officials insist that the problem isn't the roads themselves, but the amount and type of human use on them. "We eventually settled on the fact that the real risk wasn't access but *open* access," said Rob Staniland, who represented the Canadian Association of Petroleum Producers (CAPP) on the recovery team. If industrial access roads are used only by industrial operators and not for recreation, he argued, then the problems for grizzlies are considerably less. "From an industry standpoint, [we think] grizzlies are manageable with access control."

While this may be true in theory, so far it has been impossible to implement in reality. The number of registered all-terrain vehicles in Alberta has swelled from around 20,000 in 1995 to 70,000 today, most of them used for business and pleasure in what remains of Alberta's grizzly bear habitat. According to one anonymous owner of a company that provides security for industry in grizzly habitat, the protection of endangered species such as the grizzly bear has been marred by unenforced recovery and protection plans and weak provincial government policies that allow industry to police itself. The owner continues:

> I applaud Jeff Gailus for informing Albertans of our wildlife crisis. As the owner of a security guard company specializing in oilfield and industrial-road access restriction in wildlife zones, I can testify to the difficulty [of] enforcing restricted access when provincial legislation does not

provide us with the means to effectively do so. Our presence on site is frequently disregarded by citizens who ignore our attempts to limit access, and there are no laws that would enable us to stop them.

Reports of unauthorized access in endangered-species-habitat recovery zones go largely unchecked by the departments responsible for enforcement, because of staffing limitations due to underfunding, ineffective regulations and lack of enforceable laws. Steel locked gates do not work, as locks are simply cut. A few companies do hang up signs advising that access is restricted – putting responsibility on the average citizen to "do the right thing" and stay out of the area. But while these issues of gate effectiveness, access restriction and monitoring are being debated between industry and government, our wildlife is disappearing.

There are other problems with the recovery plan, too. The "priority areas" that would allow for the fewest numbers of roads, and hence the most secure habitat, are too small to ensure that a "viable and self-sustaining" population of grizzly bears is maintained across the recovery area. And the secondary areas, which are allowed to maintain road densities twice the standard threshold for grizzly bears, will be little more than mortality sinks, places were adventurous adults or dispersing subadults go to die.

There is also the little matter of the government actually adhering to the recovery plan it has adopted. The plan includes the need to designate grizzly bear priority areas, in which roads and trails accessible by motorized vehicle would be limited to the same densities used in other jurisdictions. But when government officials held stakeholder meetings to discuss how to implement access management on the ground, they were only willing to talk about managing access for four-wheel-drive *trucks,* which is a much weaker definition of "motorized vehicle" than everywhere else where access is limited to protect grizzly bears. "It is not consistent to how access affects mortality," said

CAPP's Staniland. "The recovery plan doesn't distinguish a quad trail from a highway."

Another example further undermines the faith Albertans have in the government's sincerity with respect to grizzly bear recovery. Just months after adopting the recovery plan, then Minister of Sustainable Development Ted Morton disbanded the recovery team that the plan stipulates is supposed to oversee its implementation. It's as if Morton, the minister responsible for implementing the plan, hadn't even read it. Or if he had, he didn't much care for what it said, content instead to make it up as he goes along.

All the while, the government allows the forces that threaten the grizzly bears to continue apace. The forestry industry, which already has turned 1.6 million hectares of Alberta forests into 25 million cubic metres of timber, is building more roads and creating more clear-cuts than ever. One estimate, by landscape ecologist Brad Stelfox predicts that by 2105, the forestry industry will have cleared approximately 10 million hectares, or five times the size of the four Rocky Mountain national parks.

Not to be outdone, the number of oil wells has increased exponentially since the 1950s, now numbering in excess of 90,000. It's the same story for natural gas wells, which now exceed 140,000. Those are just the ones in operation. More than 150,000 abandoned wellsites dot the landscape, too, and as industry drills 3000 wells each year, the backlog of those awaiting reclamation only grows.

It's not just the wells that are problematic, it's the roads and seismic lines that accompany them. More than 140,000 kilometres of pipelines transport the hydrocarbons these wells pump out of the ground, only slightly less than the 180,000 kilometres of roads that criss-cross the province today. All of these disturbances, all of which occur in grizzly bear habitat, are predicted to increase exponentially over the next century.

Stelfox, who has developed a computer model that uses all of this data (and more) to predict whether grizzly bear populations will thrive or die, has assessed the likelihood that grizzlies will be able to survive in southwest Alberta. "No matter what I do," he says, "I can't [develop a model that will] keep them on the landscape for more than 50 years. There's just no way."

Pissot warned the crowd at the grizzly bear workshop: "If we continue on this track, the grizzly will continue to disappear and eventually wink out. What we have today is a perpetuation of the illusion that these bears are doing okay. We have seen a suppression of information, a plethora of platitudes, and little action. Over a period when we knew grizzly bears were in trouble, we've seen continued development, increasing road densities and declining grizzly bear habitat security."

Perhaps the most chilling presentation of the day was delivered by Scott Nielsen, a University of Alberta professor who modelled the impacts of logging on grizzly populations south of Hinton and east of Jasper National Park. Surprisingly, it showed that logging plans for the area over the next 100 years would actually improve the habitat for bears by emulating the fires that once created patchy forests and more food for the animals. But the roads built to access the timber will also increase human-caused mortality rates to the point that, by 2050, the grizzly will have been extirpated from provincial lands and relegated to the relative safety of the national parks.

Despite the ominous predictions, Pissot tried to end his presentation on an upbeat note. "I've tried not to sugar-coat the picture. But that doesn't mean I'm not optimistic," he said. "The swift fox is an example of Albertans doing things right and making a difference. And I think we can maintain a healthy grizzly bear population and enjoy a healthy economy at the same time." He suggested that what we need to do is embrace the Yellowstone model. The grizzly population in and around Yellowstone National Park is the only one in the world to have been brought back from the brink of extinction, and the man who has coordinated that effort for almost 30 years was scheduled to conclude today's workshop.

The Trouble with Science

The trouble with science is that no matter how rigorous the research, no matter how many hundreds of studies draw the same conclusions, there is always someone with a vested interest in disbelieving and discrediting it. It took decades to defeat the tobacco lobby's attacks on the undeniable evidence that smoking cigarettes causes cancer. Currently, the coal and oil industries have spent millions of dollars trying to discredit what is probably the most unanimous consensus in the history of science – that the world's climate is warming and the cause is us. In Alberta, the deniers belong to the Alberta Fish & Game Association.

AFGA, as it is known in Alberta, was a late addition to the workshop agenda. When they found out there was going to be a workshop on grizzly bears, and that Jim Pissot had somehow made it onto the agenda, the AFGA executive sent their first vice-president, Quentin Bochar, to present their perspective too. But rather than stand up in front of the crowd, Bochar darted up to the lectern, mumbled a few words about having a different perspective that he didn't really want to debate right now, and then – with a nod to some invisible assistant in the back – he left as quickly as he had come.

The room darkened and a movie flashed onto the screen in the front. It was largely a series of brief interviews with hunters, guide–outfitters and other backcountry types. A line-up of talking heads, many of them wearing cowboy hats or sitting astride horses, told the camera that there are plenty of grizzly bears in Alberta, perhaps as many as 3000. The grizzlies, they asserted, needed to be hunted (by them, of course) in order to keep the province safe from these vicious carnivores. Even Minister of Sustainable Resource Development Ted Morton, who had authorized his staff to spend three million taxpayer dollars to count grizzly bears, made a cameo appearance in support of AFGA. (He later admitted during question period in the Alberta legislature that he had been out hunting with friends and had had a few "drinks" that day.)

The basis of their claim of an exploding population of grizzlies was a "Traditional Grizzly Bear Survey" that AFGA and the Willmore Wilderness Foundation were conducting. They encouraged "people who spent considerable time" in the woods to report grizzly bear sightings to a team of people who would consolidate them into a database. In just eight months, they had collected "close to five hundred bear sightings and dozens of reports of tracks where the bears were not seen." While they admitted that some people may have seen the same bears at different times, they also acknowledged "the widely held belief that for every bear that is seen, there are five to seven bears that are not seen."

The methodology seemed about as full of holes as a colander, and their conclusion – that there are thousands of bears roaming Alberta's heavily industrialized mountains and foothills – defied everything I had ever learned about grizzly bear ecology. So when I found myself behind bear biologist Michael Proctor in the lunch line, I asked him what he thought of AFGA's position. "It's quite a stretch," he said. "We don't manage moose by asking the local hunting community how many moose there are, and we shouldn't do that for grizzly bears."

As for the need to hunt grizzly bears to keep them from attacking people, well, Proctor scoffed: "There are two perfect experiments going on in the United States right now, one in Yellowstone and one in the Northern Continental Divide Ecosystem. In both cases, we've got bears coming out of the woodwork in areas that see millions of visitors and residents, and there are virtually no problems. The key isn't hunting, it's managing garbage and other attractants – and access."

While I was grilling Proctor, Pissot tracked down Bochar to see if there wasn't at least something they could agree on. After a brief conversation over a garbanzo bean salad, it became clear that they'd just have to agree to disagree about the population numbers. But Pissot was sure they could work together to protect grizzly bear habitat – if only to allow the population to grow big enough to allow hunters to shoot them – by reducing the number of roads on the landscape.

"Well," said Bochar. "We probably can't agree on that either. I like to ride my quad all over the place, and I don't really want to see any of the roads and trails closed."

The drama that unfolded at the grizzly bear workshop focused only on Alberta's bears, but a similar story is taking place on the other side of the Continental Divide, in British Columbia. Population growth, urban sprawl, roads and railways, logging, oil and gas exploration and hunting are threatening the health of the grizzly bear population in Canada's westernmost province. The biggest difference is that instead of the 800 grizzly bears remaining in a sliver of western Alberta, there are about 15,000 roaming the forests of BC. Still, the rugged terrain and increasing levels of development are conspiring, just as they have in Alberta and the US, to fragment BC's large bear population into smaller and smaller pieces, each of which is much more susceptible to decline than the larger whole.

Of 57 grizzly bear population units (GBPUs) in BC (compared to only six in Alberta), nine are listed as threatened. These threatened GBPUs are located in south and southwest BC, where human populations and urban and industrial development dominate the landscape. Four of BC's threatened GBPUs abut the US border, on the other side of which are small endangered grizzly populations protected by the US Endangered Species Act.

Although BC policy seems much more comprehensive and proactive than Alberta's, the degree of implementation is not much better. The BC government drafted a "grizzly bear conservation strategy" in 1995, but it has not been put into operation. As a first step in recovering its threatened populations, the BC government drafted a recovery plan for grizzly bears in the North Cascade Mountains in 2004. The foundation of the plan was to provide adequate secure habitat, and to augment a tiny population of fewer than 25 animals with grizzlies from other, healthier populations. To date, little if anything has been done to implement the North Cascade Grizzly Bear Recovery Plan, never mind protect BC's other small, isolated and threatened population units.

Only the US Fish & Wildlife Service has successfully begun the long process of recovering North America's beleaguered grizzly bear populations, which was why Chris Servheen was batting cleanup here at the grizzly bear workshop. In jeans and a red-and-black plaid vest, a grey handlebar moustache adorning his weathered face, he looked like a man who had spent most of his life wandering the Rocky Mountain West looking for wild animals. It had been almost two years since I'd seen him, and I was interested to hear what he might say to this crowd. He is a bureaucrat after all, one who has been through tumultuous political battles of his own through the years. I knew he had learned to keep his guard up. Instead, he opened with a salvo that I never expect to hear from his Alberta counterparts.

"Recovering grizzly bears is a social issue, not a biological one," said Servheen. "The big impediments are political. Everybody has an axe to grind. One of the reasons I have an unlisted phone number is because of how ugly it got." I looked across the room and saw Pissot nodding. Though they work on opposite sides of the political divide – Servheen as a career bureaucrat, Pissot as a career advocate – they understand each other better than perhaps anyone else in the room.

"You can't let political impediments get in the way," Servheen continued. "You can't do some things and not others. Providing habitat security and managing access are key – we closed thousands of miles of roads, for example. And it took serious government commitment, so that when difficult decisions had to be made – and they did have to be made – they were made."

Rick Bonar, a somewhat controversial biologist for Weldwood, which cuts timber in Alberta's grizzly recovery area, puts up his hand during question period. He wants to know how to manage access without removing or precluding roads. Rick sat on the grizzly bear recovery team, and was one of the more belligerent adherents to the "roads don't kill bears, people kill bears" philosophy.

"That's a Holy Grail question," said Servheen, stopping a moment to prepare an adequate response. "In the US we have what's called the Knucklehead Factor: it's always 5 or 10 per cent of the people who cause all the problems. We don't even count gated roads as closed because we can't get people to obey the closures. So if the Knucklehead Factor exists in Alberta, you can't reduce access without closing roads."

I turned to the government employees I'd been chatting with all afternoon. "Do we have the Knucklehead Factor in Alberta?" They all nodded as if their heads were on springs. "Yeah," said one, "it's everywhere."

"What we faced in the US is exactly what you're facing here in Alberta," Servheen said. "There were lots of people who didn't want it to happen. There were entire groups created to prevent it. But we did it anyway."

Albertans, meanwhile, had just received a new report on the status of their grizzly bears, which the provincial government commissioned in the hope it would help the Endangered Species Conservation Committee (ESCC) re-evaluate its earlier recommendation to list the Alberta grizzly as a threatened species. The content was predictable. The Grande Cache Population Unit boasts a significant number of bears in protected and roadless areas, but habitat conditions seem to have worsened and the population has shrunk in the last decade or so. It is hard to imagine that the ESCC recommendation will be any different this time around: stop playing games and list the Alberta grizzly as a threatened species.

Ironically, Alberta's new, disappointing population estimate, which the provincial government had hoped would find there are plenty of grizzly bears in Alberta, has prompted the Committee on the Status of Endangered Wildlife in Canada (COSEWIC) to take another look at the state of Canada's entire grizzly bear population. While the federal government does protect other species at risk at the subpopulation level, grizzly bears have always been lumped together into one big population. However, recent research in Alberta and BC indicates that bear populations on the margins are withering on the vine and may require federal protections under the Species at Risk Act.

After the workshop, during car ride home, I asked Pissot what he thought the chances were that the Alberta government would do what it will take to recover Alberta's grizzly bear population.

"Not sure," he said. "It doesn't look good, does it?"

After a moment of silence, he began to muse aloud: poll after poll shows growing public concern over the development of Alberta's remaining wild lands. Maybe we are reaching some sort of tipping point that will force the protection of the Alberta landscape not only for the grizzly but for a myriad of other species living on the edge: the stonecat, soapweed, northern long-eared bat and bull trout, for instance.

"Perhaps we can pull Alberta from the dark ages after all," he said with a wry smile. "If we can stand all the kicking and screaming."

Time for a Revolution

It is winter now, in the first month of 2010. The grizzly bears have all succumbed to the pseudo-sleep of hibernation. While the males slumber and the females nurture their cubs, politicians, bureaucrats and bear managers busily type out their plans. For the bears, these are the people and the processes that will determine whether they will live or die when warmer weather coaxes them to wake and leave the safety of their dens.

When they do, the world will be celebrating 2010 as the International Year of Biodiversity. The primary goal of these "UN International Year Ofs" is to raise awareness – in this case, awareness of the need to protect the very fabric of life on Earth, of which the grizzly bear is such an integral part. The hope is that increased understanding will help to bridge the gap between the scientists – who are telling us that human activity is causing the greatest mass extinction since the dinosaurs disappeared 65 million years ago – and the policy makers – who are all but ignoring a crisis that seems to have dropped out of sight since climate change ascended as the environmental issue of the millennium.

It has been 18 years since 150 countries, Canada first among them, signed the Convention on Biological Diversity at the 1992 Rio Earth Summit. The biodiversity convention is the other Kyoto. Designed to recognize and halt the catastrophic decline of the diversity of life on this planet, it makes the Kyoto Protocol's failed attempts to curb climate-warming greenhouse gases look like a Super Bowl victory.

The script is familiar to those who have followed our attempts to deal with climate change. In late January 2010, Ahmed Djoghlaf, executive secretary of the Convention on Biological Diversity, noted that the world has failed to fulfil the target adopted to substantially reduce the rate of loss of biodiversity by 2010. He warned that more than 100 national reports submitted to the biodiversity convention confirmed that we continue to lose biodiversity at an "unprecedented rate." Despite a national biodiversity strategy and an international reputation as an environmental champion, Canadian governments, both Liberal and Conservative, have done little to stem the tide of urban and industrial development – the main cause of extinction in Canada.

UNESCO director general Irina Bokova said we must not be discouraged by the outcomes of the UN Climate Change Conference last December in Copenhagen. Instead, she evoked the destruction of natural habitats and accelerated biodiversity loss. She warned: "We must change current trends. The future we choose for our planet is in our hands." The question is, how?

The grizzly bear, once heralded as a fierce symbol of wilderness, has become a much broader and more ironic symbol: one that now represents our domineering and ultimately destructive relationship with nature. Inaccessible wilderness was once the only place grizzly bears could survive, but it too has disappeared. With the ascendancy of industrialism, and the onset of climate change, there is virtually no place on this great blue planet that remains unmolested by *Homo sapiens industrialis*. Grizzly bears will now survive not in those places left wild, but in those places where we actively decide that they should.

Although Americans struggle to address a long list of environmental problems of their own, the ongoing success of grizzly bear recovery and management provides something of a lesson to the rest of us. The basic equation is rather simple: we need to manage the landscape in ways that allow grizzly bear populations to maintain their range and numbers. In some cases, such as Alberta, we need to allow small populations to expand so they do not dwindle away to nothing.

How to do that, as I have tried to make clear, is a rather more difficult problem in light of our rapacious appetite for natural resources. The problem is moral, not biological. The solution requires more humility and restraint than we are used to demonstrating. It also requires a political system that allows citizens to hold their political representatives accountable, something that is in short supply in Canada.

The grizzly bear is one of the most studied species in North America. Biologists tell us what they eat, where they live, how they die, how they are related to one another, and even how stressed they are from living in such close quarters with large numbers of people. Ecologists have learned much about the important role grizzlies play in the health of the natural world. They help regulate prey species, which, for instance, influences the size and health of ungulate populations. In turn, they alter the fitness of plant communities, beyond dispersing plant seeds and aerating soil so plants can regenerate, which subsequently affects the health of migratory songbirds. Grizzlies also transport nutrients, for example, by dragging the carcasses of spawning salmon into forests, where they provide protein-rich food for other animals and much-needed nitrogen to trees. The trees then provide shade for plants in the understorey, and habitat for woodpeckers and squirrels. Perhaps most important, grizzlies help to regulate the quantity and quality of the water we all need to survive. Grizzly bears, it turns out, are an indispensable part of the natural world in which we live.

We do not need any more information about bears. What we need now is to understand that the way we do business today is unsustainable. We need to stop focusing on the bears and ecosystems that we are pushing to the brink, and start finding a new and healthier way of managing ourselves.

To this end, social scientists have been exploring our attitudes and beliefs about grizzly bears, information that is likely more important to their survival than what we know about how much they eat or how they breed. The news, if you're a grizzly bear, is good. Poll after poll after poll indicates that people, in Canada and the US, overwhelmingly support the conservation and preservation of grizzly bears, no matter the cost. Even in Alberta, where money is king and restraint a sin, polls indicate that the majority of Albertans support restrictions on industrial development, on access to public lands and on hunting. You would never know it from government policy, but Albertans are even "willing to accept limits to energy development to allow for more habitat protection."

If this is the case, why is it that every reasonable assessment of the future of grizzly bears in Canada is rife with uncertainty and decline, in large part because of unrestricted industrial development, access to public lands and habitat destruction? It is, in short, a problem with how we govern ourselves.

In Canada, our governments are failing us. The roots of Canada's problem are historical. Unlike our American neighbours, the Canadian political system was born of an inherent *trust* in government. Power is centralized and there are few checks and balances. There is no separation of powers as there is in the United

States, for instance, which means the cabinet effectively controls both the legislative and the executive functions of government. As a result, Canadian laws provide maximum flexibility and a minimum of mandatory duties, including adherence to legally enforceable standards. This makes for *easy and expedient* decision-making, especially by majority governments, but it does not necessarily make for *good* decision-making.

According to David Boyd, one of Canada's most distinguished legal experts on environmental law and policy, Canada's record is one of the worst in the developed world. Our environmental legislation is weak or non-existent, and the non-binding policy mechanisms we prefer in their stead are often unenforceable. Where they do exist, the vast majority of Canada's environmental laws are undermined by their broadly discretionary nature. Laws are drafted to give governments *power* but no *obligation* to take action or meet standards. Enforcement of environmental laws is entirely discretionary and not subject to judicial review.

In other words, the government cannot be forced to enforce or even obey its own laws, whether they pertain to endangered species or drinking water.

"Some of the most basic, rudimentary [environmental] laws enacted by other nations are still absent in Canada," Boyd writes in his book *Unnatural Law*. "Canada's lack of progress in legally protecting species at risk is an international embarrassment. Canada faces serious threats to its legacy of biological diversity, although we lack the knowledge to quantify the extent of the problem." Even Canada's Biodiversity Convention Office admits that Canada is "still a long way from being able to produce a 'state of biodiversity report' that would provide a better understanding of the state of biodiversity in Canada."

To help fulfill its commitment under the Convention on Biological Diversity, the federal government passed the Species at Risk Act (SARA) in 2003. It was supposed to be the equivalent to the US Endangered Species Act, but critics say it has failed miserably. In a recent *Edmonton Journal* article, environmental journalist Ed Struzik wrote:

> But since becoming law in 2003, the Species at Risk Act (SARA) has performed more like a lamb than the lion that scientists and environmentalists had hoped it would be. They hoped it would help wildlife recover from the devastating effects of climate change, habitat loss, pollution and overharvesting.
>
> In dozens of cases, the federal government has either stalled, delayed or evaded taking legal protection for species that dwell on federal land.
>
> It has also never used the so-called "safety net," which gives it the power to protect species that may be at risk and not protected in any meaningful way in a province or territory.
>
> In fact, the federal government has sometimes fought so hard not to do anything that a Federal Court of Canada justice recently ruled that Environment Minister

Jim Prentice was in 'clear contravention of the law' in one case that is likely to apply to many others.

"It's like a death watch," says Susan Pinkus, a biologist for Ecojustice, the environmental law group that went to court on behalf of several environmental groups recently to force the government to set aside critical habitat for the greater sage grouse and for the Nooksack dace, a small fish that dwells in a handful of freshwater streams in British Columbia.

"Instead of working to protect Canada's endangered species, the federal government is working to evade the law intended to protect them."

This leaves the legal burden for protecting species at risk to the provinces and territories. But neither BC nor Alberta even have legislation protecting species at risk. Alberta's Wildlife Act, for instance, was designed decades ago to regulate hunting and fishing, but it doesn't effectively protect or recover threatened or endangered species. It enables, but does not require, the government to designate species at risk. Even when the government does, the preparation of effective recovery plans and the protection of habitat – the key elements to protecting most species at risk – are purely discretionary. In a perverse twist, the Minister of Sustainable Resource Development can reopen the trophy hunt on grizzly bears even if he decides to list them as a threatened species.

Says Geoff Scudder in his paper "Endangered Species Protection in Canada": "The Canadian government seems set on a course that will not only fail to fulfill Convention on Biological Diversity requirements but will also fall far short of the desires of an overwhelming majority of Canadians."

Perhaps the most egregious case of this is the Peary caribou, an animal found only in Canada. In the 1960s, an estimated 26,000 Peary caribou inhabited the islands of the High Arctic, but most of the animals starved to death when a series of catastrophic freeze-ups in the 1970s and 1990s prevented them from digging through the hard snow and ice to access food.

Recognizing a troubling trend, the Committee on the Status of Endangered Wildlife in Canada (COSEWIC) classified the Peary caribou as threatened in 1979. As numbers declined, it declared the animals on Banks Island and the Queen Elizabeth Islands as endangered in 1991. This status was reconfirmed when COSEWIC reassessed the Peary caribou in 2004. But despite this well-documented decline, virtually nothing has been done to help the Peary caribou recover. There are now no more than 2,000 animals left, and their prognosis is grim.

On a smaller scale, a similar story has unfolded far to the south, in Banff National Park. Scientists began reporting declines in mountain caribou populations in Banff and Jasper national parks as early as the 1950s. By the 1970s, when wolves had yet to recolonize the Bow Valley, there were only about 35 caribou in the Banff herd, which was once connected to larger populations in Jasper and British

Columbia. In the early 1990s, there were still approximately 25 individuals, but scientists were already sounding the alarm bells. By 1996, there were fewer than 10 left.

Although Parks Canada had done nothing for its ailing Banff caribou population, Environment Canada, with the blessing of Parliament, listed them and all other southern mountain caribou as a threatened species in 2000. Unfortunately, despite a legal obligation to develop a recovery plan and identify critical habitat within three years of listing, neither of these critical steps was ever taken. It wasn't until 2002, with just five caribou left, that Parks Canada even began monitoring the state of their caribou population.

The end of the story is as predictable as it is tragic. Parks Canada started to implement some common-sense management actions in 2002. However, their efforts were "a penny short and a second too late," according to University of Montana biologist Mark Hebblewhite, who has studied these caribou for more than 20 years. In April 2009, an avalanche north of Lake Louise wiped out every last one of Banff's four remaining caribou.

"This is one of the first large mammal extinctions…in a [Canadian] national park in a long time," he told CBC when it happened. "They kind of fell through the cracks. There's all these rules and policies about SARA and it's all very confusing, but at the end of the day, the caribou in Banff fell through administrative cracks. I would say adequate funding and resources weren't really directed to them when they really needed it."

Unless there is a significant reform – even a revolution – in how Canada manages its plants and animals, and the habitat upon which we all depend, we can expect this fate for grizzly bears, too.

The real obstacle to reforming the system, says David Boyd, is the dominance of short-term economic interests. Economic activity, particularly industrial, is the biggest threat to most species at risk. Effectively protecting these species often entails limiting human activities to within confines dictated by nature.

Provincial governments, whose revenues often depend on increasing industrial development, are loath to adopt meaningful species at risk legislation. Furthermore, the federal government seems uninterested in interfering in what it considers a provincial issue. Even in our national parks, where protecting the environment is supposed to be the "first priority," economic interests out-compete environmental interests at every turn. At least this certainly seems to be the case in Banff.

This seems an aberration to me, but it is a reflection of how Canadians perceive the government's role in protecting the environment. Would we tolerate such a flippant attitude toward, say, ferreting out and prosecuting terrorists or child molesters? Would we want the government to be able to decide, on a whim, whether or not to prosecute a suspect when evidence suggests the suspect has committed an atrocious crime? If not, why would we allow governments, especially governments that are so heavily influenced by corporations, such latitude in the protection of our water and air and wildlife?

Still, when I put this argument to some of my Canadian friends, they balk at the notion of investing the courts with the power to hold governments accountable by forcing them to obey their own laws. Even one friend who is a committed grizzly bear conservationist, and well aware of the shortcomings in the current system, was reluctant to embrace what he perceived as an American system founded on "litigiousness and confrontation."

What I think he yearns for, like all of us, is a Canadian society based on polite and peaceful coexistence. Don't we endure enough confrontation already? Isn't there another way to maintain "peace, order and good government"? Do we really need to refer the protection of our environment to the courts? Can't we do it ourselves?

The evidence suggests the answer is no. If there is a more collaborative and conciliatory way to protect nature, its foundation will be transparent and enforceable laws and policies that hold citizens, corporations and governments accountable for their actions. The rule of law is the foundation of Western democracies, and grizzly bears deserve its protection as much as people do.

What worries me the most is that despite all the evidence to the contrary, Canadians tend to overestimate the degree to which their governments are looking after the environment. Perhaps it is our inherent trust in the government, or perhaps it is our penchant to live up to our reputation as overly polite conflict-avoiders. Whatever the reason, we give our governments far more credit than they are due. For instance, a recent poll indicated that while most Albertans admit to being uninformed about grizzly bears, they also believe that grizzly bear populations are managed sustainably, when in fact they are in deep trouble. This misconception is a problem, of course, but governments like to reinforce it to look good for the next election.

I have tried to deconstruct this illusion of success over the years, but it is difficult to do. Government officials control most of the cards and they hold them close to their chests. And their well-paid spokespeople are as slick as *Thank You for Smoking*'s Nick Naylor.

I spoke with Dave Ealey, a registered professional biologist and senior "issues manager" for the Ministry of Sustainable Resource Development (SRD), which oversees grizzly bear management in Alberta. When I asked him how much of the 1990 management plan was actually implemented, and whether it was effective or not, he was unwilling to answer the questions. Eventually, Ealey told me that Alberta has "done very well for bears over the last 15 years," citing inadequate technology and lack of information for any potential shortfalls.

"Why hasn't the government listed the grizzly bear as a threatened species yet?"

"We manage the landscape as if it's a working landscape, as opposed to a landscape where there's nothing happening," said Ealey. "An important part of the value of this landscape is to the resource economy."

"You're a biologist," I finally said. "How can you say such things speaking as a professional biologist?"

"I'm not speaking as a biologist," he said. "I'm speaking on behalf of SRD."

It's easy enough to blame governments and their henchmen, of course, but ultimately it's not just them who are failing us. We are failing ourselves. The only way to turn things around in Canada is to begin paying attention to the environmental politics that whirl around us like snowflakes in an East Coast storm. We must incorporate these politics into the way we live our lives and especially into the way we vote.

Although climate change captures most of the headlines these days, the grizzly bear is trying to tell us there are other problems afoot. Our governments are beholden to corporate interests, and they have become unresponsive and unaccountable beasts.

You are not paying attention, Bear Mary and Bear 56 are telling us. You are not taking care. Wake up. It is time for a revolution.

Further Reading

Boyd, David. *Unnatural Law: Rethinking Canadian Environ-
    mental Law and Policy.* Vancouver: UBC Press, 2003.

Canadian Press. Conservationists worried about Parks
    Canada's plan to attract more visitors. *The Toronto Star,*
    January 5, 2010, travel section.

Fluker, Shaun. Ecological Integrity in Canada's National
    Parks: The False Promise of Law. 29 *Windsor Review of
    Legal and Social Issues,* 2010 [forthcoming].

Henton, Darcy. Nearly all black bears deaths in parks
    caused by humans. *Edmonton Journal,* January 13, 2010,
    technology section.

Herrero, Stephen. *Bear Attacks: Their Causes and Avoidance.*
    New York: Nick Lyons Books/Winchester Press, 1985.

Leopold, Aldo. *A Sand County Almanac, and Sketches Here
    and There.* London and New York: Oxford University
    Press, 1968. First published 1949.

Marty, Sid. *The Black Grizzly of Whiskey Creek.* Toronto:
    McClelland & Stewart, 2008.

McCracken, Harold. *The Beast that Walks like a Man: The
    Story of the Grizzly Bear.* London: Oldbourne Press, 1947.

McNamee, Thomas. *The Grizzly Bear*. New York: Knopf, 1984.

Murray, John A. *The Great Bear: Contemporary Writings on the Grizzly*. Anchorage: Alaska Northwest Books, 1992.

Peacock, Doug, and Andrea Peacock. *The Essential Grizzly: the Mingled Fates of Men and Bears*. Guilford, Conn.: Lyons Press, 2006.

Rockwell, David. *Giving Voice to Bear: North American Indian Rituals, Myths, and Images of the Bear*. Niwot, Colo.: Roberts Rinehart Publishers, 1991.

Schullery, Paul. *Lewis and Clark among the Grizzlies: Legend and Legacy in the American West*. Guilford, Conn.: Falcon, 2002.

Scudder, Geoff. 1999. "Endangered Species Protection in Canada." Conservation Biology 13(5): 965.

Searle, Rick. *Phantom Parks: The Struggle To Save Canada's National Parks*. Toronto: Key Porter Books, 2000.

Shepard, Paul, and Barry Sanders. *The Sacred Paw: The Bear in Nature, Myth and Literature*. New York: Viking, 1985.

Struzik, Ed. "It's like a death watch": Environmentalists say Canada is dithering despite clear evidence showing many species in decline. *Edmonton Journal,* January 15, 2010, opinion section.

About the Author

Jeff Gailus has spent hundreds of hours observing grizzlies and guiding people through bear habitat. His poignant journalism and commitment to conservation have earned him a Doris Duke Conservation Fellowship, a Story of the Year award from the Associated Collegiate Press and numerous shortlistings and honourable mentions for his magazine writing. He recently received Canada Council for the Arts and Alberta Foundation for the Arts grants to work on *Original Griz*, an environmental history of the Great Plains grizzly. His follow-up to *The Grizzly Manifesto* will be *The Wolf Manifesto: In Defence of* Canis lupus, to be published by RMB in Fall 2011.

Denying the Source

The Crisis of First Nations Water Rights

Merrell-Ann S. Phare

The demands for access to waters that First Nations depend upon are intense and growing. Oil and gas, mining, ranching, farming and hydro development all require enormous quantities of water, and each brings its own set of negative impacts to the rivers, lakes and groundwater sources that are critical to First Nations. Climate change threatens to make matters even worse. This book is a call to respect the water rights of First Nations, and in doing so, to create a new water ethic in Canada and beyond.

ISBN-13: 978-1897522615

The Weekender Effect

Hyperdevelopment in Mountain Towns

Robert William Sandford

As cities continue to grow at unprecedented rates, more and more people are looking for peaceful, weekend retreats in mountain or rural communities. More often than not, these retreats are found in and around resorts or places of natural beauty. As a result, what once were small towns are fast becoming mini-cities, complete with expensive housing, fast food, traffic snarls and environmental damage, all with little or no thought for the importance of local history, local people and local culture. The Weekender Effect is a passionate plea for considered development in these communities and for the necessary preservation of local values, cultures and landscapes.

ISBN-13: 978-1897522103

RMB saved the following resources by printing the pages of this book on chlorine-free paper made with 100% post-consumer waste:

Trees · 8, fully grown

Water · 3,483 gallons

Solid Waste · 211 pounds

Greenhouse Gases · 723 pounds

Calculations based on research by Environmental Defense and the Paper Task Force. Manufactured at Friesens Corporation.